Between the Acts

Between the Acts

Lives of homosexual men 1885–1967

Edited by Jeffrey Weeks and Kevin Porter

Rivers Oram Press
London and New York

Published in 1998 by
Rivers Oram Press
144 Hemingford Road, London N1 1DE

Distributed in the USA by
New York University Press
Elmer Holmes Bobst Library
70 Washington Square South
New York, NY10012–1091

Set in Garamond by TNJ Design Associates, Romsey, Hants
and printed in Great Britain by
T.J. International Ltd, Padstow, Cornwall

First published in 1991
Second edition copyright © 1998 Jeffrey Weeks and Kevin Porter

British Library Cataloguing in Publication Data
A catalogue record for this book is available from the British Library

ISBN 1 85489 092 1 (cloth)
ISBN 1 85489 093 X (paperback)

Contents

Preface to the second edition

Once published, books take on lives of their own. They are open to interpretation and misinterpretation, use and abuse. Authors lose control, and that is healthy—especially for a book of this sort, for it has many voices and covers a long and often painful history. Now history has changed—with luck, for the better—so we see the past in a different light. Each period has different ways of making sense of the past. Meanings change. Events take on a new significance. We live in a different world from the ones reconstructed in this book. Nothing can be exactly the same again. The echoes are important: across the chasm of time, we can hear familiar tunes. But we have to sing them in our own way.

This book is therefore both a fragment of our history and a marker for how things have changed. We attempted to record individual stories, to honour those who lived in difficult times, morally and culturally, but survived, sometimes with great pain but often with enormous pleasure and growing pride in their lives and achievements. We also wanted to add new elements to our collective memory, to demonstrate that our lives were part of a history of many individual lives, in some ways like ours, in other ways quite different. The history of homosexuality is always a history, simultaneously, of identity and difference, of what we have in common, and of what separates us. We glimpse, through the mists of history, part of what we are, but we also recognise that some things, and perhaps we ourselves, have changed beyond recognition. Our history has changed because of what those who came before us did, but also because of what we have done in a rapidly changing world that we are now making for ourselves.

The stories in this book were recorded in 1978. They were first published in this form at the end of the first decade of the HIV/AIDS crisis, a crisis unimaginable in its horror and extent when the first interviews were done. Now the world has changed again. HIV and AIDS still relentlessly cause pain and loss, yet, as we write, there are signs that HIV may be on the way to becoming a chronic, but manageable disease, as new drugs offer hope. The devastation of the gay communities in many western countries has happened, but the communities—friendships, networks, institutions, personal and collective narratives—have survived, and in many ways been strengthened by experience. New possibilities have opened up in the wake of the epidemic, which seemed impossible when our subjects were young, and even when we completed this book; new stories can now be told.

Ken Plummer has written about the importance of sexual stories[1] in the following terms:

> we live in a world of sexual stories....Society itself may be seen as a textured but seamless web of stories emerging everywhere through interaction....Sexual stories are part of this and are also as old as human time. But in this late modern world—at century's end, at the fin de siècle, at the turn of the millennium—they seem to have gained an unusual power and prominence.

Since the emergence of the modern gay and lesbian movement in the late 1960s, there has been an explosion of sexual story telling. The most characteristic form of story telling in the immediate wake of the new gay politics related to coming out: as people gained confidence to speak out, to reveal what was generally covert (and illegal), to share common experiences, they helped to weave a web of narratives that have become a vital part of what we now call the lesbian and gay community. We recognise ourselves in other people's narratives; they become part of our lives. Many of the life stories in this book are, in part, coming out stories. They help us to understand the complex ways in which individual and collective identities are formed, tested and lived.

We would like to argue that we are now moving into a new phase of story telling, where the stories currently being told are about our different ways of life: about intimate relationships, 'friends as family', 'families of choice', love, partnerships, loss and death. We no longer need simply to assert our presence: 'we are everywhere'. We have become more concerned with the ethos and values that sustain our ways of life.

Again, in the life stories of this book, we see many precedents for all this. We may often feel we live in a world where the journeys are a little uncertain and the maps are indecipherable, but from this book, and others like it, we can see that others have pursued their travels with a similar lack of guidance, and have survived and flourished.

Somehow, then, we have to hold on to a dual perspective: a sense of a collective history which made possible what we are; and a sense of what is different for those living now, and those who will come after us. Memory is a fickle thing; if we fail to remember the past, we may well be doomed to repeat it. But if we just live in the past, we cannot grasp the future.

We offer this book again to our readers in the belief that the lives recorded here can provide a bridge between a past that is fast fading and a future still to be made.

Most of those who offered their memories for this book had died by the time the book was published. We can sadly record one more recent death: Trevor Thomas ('An academic life') died on 27 May 1993. Angus Suttie, who worked on the early editing of the book, died on 17 June 1993.

Their lives live on in this book.

Note

1. Ken Plummer, *Telling Sexual Stories: Power, Change and Social Worlds*, Routledge, 1995, pp.6–7

Preface and acknowledgments to the first edition

This book is based on a unique collection of interviews with older homosexual men, which throws new light on a period when male homosexuality was illegal in Britain. This is the period 'between the acts', the Criminal Law Amendment Act of 1885, which finally made all sexual activities between men illegal, and the Sexual Offences Act of 1967, which partially decriminalised such activities under a number of severe restrictions.

The interviews were conducted during 1979 by one of the editors, Jeffrey Weeks, as part of a research project, based at Essex University, designed to explore the development of homosexual subcultures and identities in Britain. The project was funded by the then Social Science Research Council for a period of eighteen months. The grant was not extended after a major reduction in SSRC funds following the Conservative election victory in May 1979.

We are publishing these interviews now, more than ten years after they were conducted, because of a growing interest in lesbian and gay history, and following a series of requests over the years from interested researchers for access to this material. Most of the people interviewed in this volume have, sadly, died over the past decade. The material presented here is, therefore, an unrepeatable source of evidence for a way of life that has now changed beyond recognition.

Apart from one or two short extracts in other publications, none of this interview material has ever been published before. It is an exceptional resource, because almost all the original twenty-five interviews were with men born between the 1880s and the 1920s. They were able, therefore, to provide insights into a crucial period when the documentary sources are limited, either because they came down to us through notorious scandals, or through the memoirs and biographies of literary homosexuals. These interviews, on the contrary, are with ordinary people from a variety of class, occupational and geographical backgrounds, and with differing political and social attitudes.

The interviews do not, of course, reflect the whole range of male homosexual experience. There are, for example, no members of ethnic minority communities represented, or anyone who lived in Scotland or Ireland for any length of time. For a number of reasons there are also few accounts of long-term partnerships, despite plentiful evidence that such relationships existed. This is partly a result of the truncated nature of the original project. It is also a result of the inherent difficulty of obtaining a representative sample of people when they had grown accustomed, in a period of illegality, to keeping their personal needs and public personae completely separate. Nevertheless, the interviewees are able to provide exceptional insights into the complex, varied and uneven fashion by which homosexually inclined people made sense of their needs and desires, and fashioned for themselves manageable social, and sexual, ways of life.

The original twenty-five subjects were identified in a number of ways. Some were by the late 1970s active in gay organisations, particularly the Campaign for Homosexual Equality (CHE) and volunteered their collaboration. Others read of the project in the gay press and offered themselves for interview. An advertisement in *The Times* produced three responses, but only one genuine respondent, who was interviewed. The initial contacts then generated a snowball effect, as interviewees recommended their friends for interview.

This book represents a selection only of those original twenty-five interviews. The fifteen included in this book offer a series of over-lapping and complementary portraits which, we believe, present a vivid impression of male homosexual life in the earlier part of this century as it was recalled in later life by active participants.

What are included here are edited versions of the original interviews. On average, each individual was interviewed for two to two-and-a-half hours, sometimes for considerably longer. Some were interviewed more than once. The transcripts of all these interviews run to hundreds of pages. It would not be possible to include all this material, rich as it often is. We have attempted, however, in the editing, to be fully truthful to the original interviews, and to include as wide a range of experiences as possible.

It should be noted that some of the names given here are pseudonyms. This is at the specific request of the interviewees, who gave freely of their memories and recollections in 1978-9 on condition that their confidentiality would be respected. Similarly, some identifying details have also been changed. No attempt has been made to up-date the interviews, and comments about the situation as it was perceived in 1979, and references to institutions now long gone (including the newspaper *Gay News*), have been kept in as appropriate.

Although the interviews were conducted by one of the two editors, the final work is a fully collaborative effort by both, who were involved together in all stages of its preparation.

We owe many thanks to a number of people for their contribution to this book. Our first debt is to Mary McIntosh whose strong backing for the profit ensured its original funding by the SSRC, and who gave unstinted support while the interviews and the complementary documentary research were being conducted. Ken Plummer as ever gave indispensable moral and intellectual support. Janet Parkin Hussain transcribed the original interviews with her usual skill and speed. The edited interviews in this book were typed swiftly and efficiently by The Typing Pool. Angus Suttie contributed to the editing of the interviews at an early stage.

But our greatest debt is to the gay men featured in this book who gave so freely and generously of their time, and have had to wait so long for their memories and experiences to be validated. We dedicate this book to them.

Introduction

In this book we are concerned with the lives of homosexual men in the period 'between the acts', the years between 1885 and 1967 when all forms of male homosexual activity in Britain were illegal.

In 1885 the Labouchère Amendment to the Criminal Law Amendment Act brought all forms of homosexuality between men within the scope of the criminal law, and made them illegal, whether conducted in public or private. Homosexuality had scarcely been legal before then, but the new enactment represented a symbolic shift, chasing even the minor misdemeanours of the flesh into the deepest privacy of the bedroom, and providing, in the famous phrase which ever thereafter clung to the Labouchère Amendment, a 'blackmailer's charter'.

This was the situation that prevailed until 1967, when the Sexual Offences Act partially decriminalised male homosexual activities: as long as they were in private (which was strictly defined), between those over twenty-one, excluding people in the armed services and the merchant navy, and in England and Wales only. But limited as the changes were, they represented the end of an era in homosexual history. This was a period of eighty-two years when homosexuals, women as well as men, inhabited what was in effect, in a famous cliché, a 'twilight world'.

These years between the acts formed the crucible in which lesbian and gay identities were forged. This is not the place to rehearse what was a complex history, or to go over the controversies about the implications of that history. Those interested will find a full discussion elsewhere (for example in Jeffrey Weeks, *Coming Out* [1]). The important point here is that homosexually inclined people were forced to come to terms with their desires, construct their personal and social identities, build relationships and discover new ways of life in a situation of illegality, prejudice, ignorance and social hostility.

Some of that experience is now well documented. We have detailed and vivid pictures of the life and loves and disasters of the first major victim of Labouchère, Oscar Wilde. We know more and more about the homosexual lives of the literary intellectuals of the next generations: E. M. Forster, Lytton Strachey, the hangers-on of Bloomsbury, J. R. Ackerley and so on. We have had novels and scandalous memoirs and films that have tried to capture some of the flavour of this period. Most recently we have begun to see the emergence of oral histories, notably those emanating from the Hall Carpenter Archive, *Walking after Midnight* [2] and *Inventing Ourselves*.[3]

This book differs from the published biographies in concentrating on the unknown, the unfamous, and often isolated, who lived their homosexuality as best they could, in difficult circumstances. It differs from the Hall Carpenter books in concentrating on the life stories of older gay men, those born between the 1880s and the 1920s.

All life stories are reconstructions, attempts to make sense of a complex reality, to provide a narrative structure for oneself as well as for others. Within themselves these interviews are not always entirely consistent or coherent. Individual memories are not always accurate. We have not attempted to iron out these inconsistencies or impose our own coherence. As editors, nevertheless, we have inevitably been selective, and therefore have in turn helped shape the material.

This selection process is true, however, of all historical source material. We believe that the individuals, whose lives are presented here, offer insights into both their own lives and the milieu in which they lived. Their recollections provide unique pathways into the diversity of homosexual lifestyles in the earlier part of the century.

Diversity is a key, if rather ambiguous term, when exploring the history (or histories) of homosexuality. At the most fundamental level of social organisation there are major differences between the developments of the lesbian and gay male identities and cultures: within the common framework of the privileging of heterosexuality and the denial of homosexuality, men and women have separate, if often intricately related histories. This book concentrates on men. But even here there are huge differences in experience, knowledge and ways of life, the result of the interplay of definition and self-definition through which identities are constructed.

On the one hand, there are the common forces of social regulation that provide the essential context, and ultimate limits, for the shaping of viable identities: legal codes, medical interventions, religious pressures, popular prejudices and so on, which defined the boundaries between the acceptable and the unacceptable, the permitted and the illicit. The interviews in this book provide plentiful examples of all these factors. Trevor, for example, illustrates vividly the impact of the law on an individual life. Thomas shows the power of guilt and a religious vocation in thwarting sexual happiness. Barry shows how the hypocrisies of England encouraged a life in partial exile. Fred's story portrays the effect of anxiety and fear in denying the realisation of an individual's deepest needs.

On the other hand, as these same life stories simultaneously demonstrate, individuals are able to find the materials to shape their own lives, and to define in a positive manner their own identities, individually and collectively, against all the odds. These life stories illustrate the personal needs, constantly erupting and changing, the family circumstances, the chance encounters, the occupational limitations and opportunities, the literary and intellectual influences, the individual courage through which these lives and identities were shaped.

What comes out strongly in the majority of the interviews is that, despite the limitations under which these people inevitably lived, they nevertheless rose to the challenge and developed fulfilling lives. The overwhelming impression is of a triumph of individual courage and endurance against the odds.

Certain experiences were, of course, common to all these lives. Several of the interviewees refer to the small body of writing on homosexuality that was then available: the work of the socialist and supporter of homosexual rights (and himself homosexual), Edward Carpenter; the writings of the pioneering sexologist, Havelock Ellis, and of his co-author in the first 'scientific' British study of homosexuality, the poet and essayist J. A. Symonds. Writers such as these provided a vocabulary through which homosexually inclined people could give meaning to their feelings, and recognise that they were not the only such individuals in the world. The explanations offered in such books (for example, that homosexuals constituted a third or 'intermediate' sex, or were a biological anomaly) may not accord with contemporary assumptions, but at the time they provided for some a way of understanding difference that proved potent in shaping emergent sexual identities.

It was, however, through contact with others that most people were able to make sense of their feelings, and to begin to forge viable identities. The interviews illustrate the existence of an already complex and widespread homosexual culture, with its own mores and rituals, language and institutions, meeting places and sexual practices. In a climate of illegality the most common places for meeting people were public spaces, such as parks, and public lavatories. But there were also pubs and clubs, particularly in London, where homosexuals gathered. Some of these provided a focus for various forms of prostitution, from straight cash transactions to more elaborate, long-term relationships where money was but one element. The interviewees provide vibrant images of the ways of life that developed in this culture, and how it shaped their own responses.

Individuals react, of course, in their different ways, depending on a host of factors. Class, for example, subtly shaped lives. For some, like Gregory from an upper-middle-class background, it provided opportunities for an early (if tacit) acceptance of his life-long relationship by family and friends. On the other hand, Thomas, from a similar background, felt constrained by his family's very respectability. Fred was effectively trapped by his working-class background, whereas John escaped it and made his homosexuality a ladder to the middle class.

Just as it would be misleading to ignore class divisions, and other factors such as geography, it would be wrong to see the long period before 1967 as monolithic or monochrome. The war years, for instance, both First and Second World Wars, led to a significant change in social behaviour, vividly described by Fred (the First World War) and Sam (the Second). The scandals in the early 1950s, then the *Wolfenden Report*, followed by the ten-year struggle to change the law, heralded a new period (though not one that was always perceived positively, or at all, by the people interviewed here).

Politics sometimes intertwined with homosexuality, either in a specific homosexual context (Gregory, for example, was a member of the earliest organisation campaigning discreetly to change the law in the 1920s) or in the more dramatic context of the anti-apartheid struggles in South Africa (Cecil). On the whole, however, before the early 1970s no one made the explicit links between attitudes towards homosexuality and social and political change that were to become commonplace from then on. Several of the subjects of this book did become involved in the gay movement after 1970 (David, Barry, Fred, Trevor, Roy and Sam), and are able, from that perspective, to reflect on the changes that have taken place. It would be fair to say, however, that again there is a range of views displayed here. While David and Cecil remain firmly committed to socialist politics, Barry sees himself as resolutely conservative.

The life stories presented here, then, offer a range of experiences, from the gregariousness of Sam to the chosen loneliness of Norman, from the respectability of Gregory to the career prostitution of Tony. They do not exhaust the diversity of the male homosexual world as it developed in the early decades of the century. We hope, however, that these interviews capture some of the richness and resilience of individual lives as well as the pain and oppressiveness of the years 'between the Acts'.

Notes

1. *Coming Out: Homosexual Politics in Britain from the Nineteenth Century to the Present*, second revised and updated edition, London, Quartet, 1990.
2. Hall Carpenter Archive, *Walking After Midnight*, London, Routledge, 1990.
3. Hall Carpenter Archive, *Inventing Ourselves*, London, Routledge, 1989.

1 A soldier's life

Gerald was born in 1892 in Norfolk. His mother died when he was four and so he lived with his grandparents and his father until the age of ten when he was sent away to an industrial school. He fought in the army throughout the First World War and it was whilst in the army that he met Phil, his lover of seven years. He stayed in the army more or less until 1942 when he retired through ill health. But his connections with the army continued into old age. After retiring he worked on the staff of one of the armed services officers clubs. When interviewed he was living alone in a bedsitter in Kensal Rise, North-West London.

I was born on 31 May 1892 in Fakenham in Norfolk. My mother died when I was four years of age. From then I went to live with my grandfather and grandmother. My father lived there at the same time. When I was about ten years of age I sort of went haywire, as it were. And of course my grandmother couldn't stand it as far as I can make out to the way I look at it now, so they put me away in this industrial school. I went to what they called the East London Industrial School in Lewisham. From that industrial school was, well, the start of all this, my homosexual life.

You had your 'friend' at the age of twelve, fourteen. I mean to say, you've probably read books on this, as regards boys in dormitories and all that, well that's the sort of atmosphere I was at. When I came out of the school I went to a farm. There was a couple of the boys there, and we used to live in the loft on top of the stables, three of us together. And we had our fun there.

It's funny, it automatically came, you couldn't avoid it. You came together.

When I actually realised that I was, shall we say, abnormal in my estimation, I wondered what was happening. Then I went in the army in 1914, and that was the first time I actually got seduced by a soldier, it was a sergeant. It was then I realised that I was that way. Ever since, my life has gone that way. That was the first contact I had with anybody, you know, from what they call, put it bluntly, from bumming. Before, it was just playing. In the army you get no chance for very much. It all had to be done in a moment. I don't know whether this person actually took advantage of me for being a young boy, I was only a youngster, eighteen, twenty in those days.

But you see, in the period of my life during '14, I was associated with a young lady. I think it was somewhere in the region of about 1916 or '17. I came home on leave periodically, and between times I was making an allotment to her mother, through her daughter, 'cos we were going to get married. When I came home the lot had gone. The whole concern. Come home, they'd disappeared. I made enquiries of neighbours next door and they said well, sorry, but as far as we know they're in Sheffield you see. I'd sent allotment on for furniture and all that sort of thing. In that period somewhere in the region of about £250 was quite a bit of money. I was drawing practically no pay in the army, you know, it was all going in the allotment, because at that period I thought a lot of my girlfriend and ever since then, of course, the whole thing went haywire. The feminine sex went right out of my life. Okay, I'll go and have a drink with a lady, a woman and that sort of thing but, as for anything else, oh no. I've got no sexual feeling, that's lost.

At that time there was no talk about homosexuality. Not the slightest. I don't think it was obvious to myself at that period, I was only about eighteen or twenty. At that age, I probably didn't realise the significance of it. I just did it. But I thought that married life, within myself, was the proper thing to do, although I had experience of the other side.

I only met one other homosexual in the army. That was at Le Havre in 1917. We was on the boat coming home. I don't know how these things work, whether it's through the conversation, or whether it's the attitude of the individual concerned, but we seemed to come together, see. All of a sudden his arm was round my neck and this, that and the other, and then, of course, one thing led to another. And that was Phil, my affair that I had for seven years. When I come out of the army we stuck together. I was living at the time in Ilford. I rejoined the army in 1920, then I went out to Germany. I was living with Phil at the same time and I saw him when I came home on leave and we kept a flat together. I was in the army because the army was my life at that period. He was somebody just like a wife to come home to.

There was no sexual contact with anybody in the services. The simple reason is, I got promoted to sergeant from corporal. As you're getting promotions, you couldn't take no chances. I had several chances mind you, with two or three different private soldiers I knew. You can gauge 'em, but the point is, when you come and look at it, you say to yourself, well is it mind over matter? You know, you say to yourself, no I musn't. You're jeopardising your chances, because if something happened you're going to get a court martial.

For example, we used to have officers coming down for training, NCOs from different regiments. And there was this particular Regimental Sergeant I never forget. He came from the Guards. Of course, the accommodation wasn't sufficient so they had to put 'em up in here. I had an arrangement with this Regimental Sergeant, who shared my room. The arrangement was, I would allow my batman to clean his gear and all that sort of business. He'd pay him. I said, yes, carry on mate. And the boy was quite agreeable to do it. Well the first couple of days it was all right. Then one day, when I was Orderly Sergeant, I was in the canteen, and all of a sudden somebody come to me. He said, your batman wants to see you at the door. So I went out. Okay. Goes out. What's wrong? I knew there was something wrong because that boy was really agitated. Actually, he was crying. So I said, what's the matter, lad? He said, the Sergeant interfered with me. I said, what? Come on, explain it. He said, he wanted me to do the buttons on his fly, flies of his trousers.

He said, well the Sergeant never seen anything wrong with that. Well that's quite true, the boy didn't realise. And when the Sergeant turned round of course he tried to do the other. Of course the boy just left him and came straight over to the canteen. I said, right, come on. Being Orderly Sergeant of the day my duty was to go straight to the Sergeants' Mess, to the Regimental Sergeant Major. I explained the situation to him. I said look lad, I said, now you tell the RSM exactly what you told me, word for word or as near as you can. He had to hear the boy give his evidence. Of course that led to a court martial. He got stripped in two years.

The point was, you see, myself, being a homosexual. How do you think I felt ...? There was nothing I could do, I couldn't protect him. I had to look after number one. See, I couldn't let the world know that I was homosexual, not in the army. Otherwise what was going to happen?

During this period Phil had gone into the plastering business and he was earning good money. Everything was okay for the seven years. We had quite a happy life together. We done the housework between us. We shared everything fifty-fifty. If I saw the stove wanted cleaning, I'd clean the stove. If he saw the chest of drawers want polishing, he'd polish the chest of drawers. I used to go out about half-past eight in the morning, and he'd go out probably earlier, somewhere about half-past-seven. On average I was home about half-past-five, he came home about half-past-six. Whoever came home first made the meal. This was up to 1926, 1927. That's when we parted.

I don't think our friends or family knew, yet they had a very good suspicion. Phil and I often talked about it, only he said well, he says, as long as we love each other, what's it to do with other people? And that was the true situation. We were faithful to each other. It wasn't a case of if he wanted to bring somebody home, he'd bring 'em home, there was nothing like that. We'd probably have our sex once a week, once a fortnight, all according to the mood we were in.

Then, we went out one night, I'll never forget, we went out one night. We went to a club, the Quebec Club in Piccadilly. It was a gay club at that time. We hadn't been in there two minutes, when, all of a sudden, up comes this other chap .... They kiss each other and all that sort of business. I thought to myself, well I don't know, they're getting a bit too close together in their conversation and this, that and the other. I got a bit annoyed. One thing led to another, and this chap turned round, he said, good gracious alive, he says, Gerald darling, don't you know? he said. I knew Phil long before you knew her. Well, of course, that aggravated it, and then — bang, bang, bang — all of a sudden there was that one climax. That was it. I left the flat, I left the flat to him.

I went to Sheffield, then I went back into the army, and didn't come back to London till 1942. Then I got this job in the military club. I was there for about another twenty odd years, until well 1962 or '61. I could say near enough since 1962, when I went up to Sheffield, I don't think I had much actual homosexual life, although I was homosexual. A lot of people think if you're homosexual you're out looking for it all the time. But if you are a genuine homosexual you don't.

See, some of these lustful people, I call 'em egoists, go out looking for sex. Most of them are doing it for what they can get out of it. They're what they call renters. They're not homosexuals. They say, you give me five pound, I'll come home with you. I've had it times without number. You pick up somebody, okay, you feel like having a bit of fun. You say, I'll give you a pound. Okay, pick 'em up. They don't want a pound, they want five. And they won't let you touch 'em. They probably want to knock you from here to there. I've come across several people like that. Once you get caught like that, you don't get caught twice. I've never paid for it in my life. Never will do.

The only sex I had was one night stands when I was on leave staying at the leave hostel of the army. Well you'd go in the bar down there, you'd have a drink, you'd get talking to people, that's the only way you can find out. You wanted it to happen. You hope it's going to happen. And then probably nothing happens! But if you do meet, there is always ample opportunity in them places, because every man has his own cubicle. There's no bother about anybody getting into trouble. That's the only chance you had for sex, when you came home on leave like that.

I don't suppose they ever had any sex contact in the barracks. 'Cos they daren't.

I don't agree with cottaging. You go down to the toilets and you stand in the pedestal there. Somebody comes and stands next to you. First thing he does is butchers looking over the pedestal. I just turn round and say, what the bloody hell are you looking at? Then I walks out. Just let them know that I'm not playing. I mean to say, you get a plainclothes policeman standing there, you don't know who's who. I've purposely listened to some of those cases and that is what's happened. Piccadilly, Charing Cross, Waterloo Station. Homosexual and caught in the cubicle, two of them in the cubicle. See they're idiots aren't they? They're daft. I mean if you're going to have sex, have sex and enjoy it. In the proper way and the proper thing of it. Not with lust. Have it with love. Have it with the real feeling of it. Okay, even if it's a one-night stand.

I get the feeling of sex, even at my age now. But I let the other man have his love feeling as well. Of course, with me I couldn't come. I'm dried up, put it that way. But I still get a feeling of having the real connection. I always let him have his fulfilment in the proper way. Sometimes you get people come along and they're one-sided. All they want is you to relieve them. They're not interested in your feelings. Which is wrong. Well it is selfishness.

I left the army after twenty-one years because that is the end of the term, the normal army contract. I don't know what happens today, but in the army in that period, if you wanted to stay after twenty-one years, you were demoted. I don't know why. They think you're past it. It's only red tape. Although when I rejoined the army yet again during 1940, when I took over the physical instructors' training class, they gave me my rank straight away!

I finally left in February or March 1942 because I went sick. The doctor examined me, because I was getting short of breath. It was diagnosed as TB, and they sent me to the army TB hostel in Kent. I automatically got discharged from the army there on grounds of ill health. I'm still drawing that pension now. Leaving the army was a big wrench. For the first five or six months after I come out I didn't like the idea of being told what to do. I was always used to telling somebody else what to do!

It was then I went to work for the military club. That was more my environment. I was with the military people. I was here for twenty odd years, to 1961. I lived in.

This is where Peter, my nephew, comes into the story. He was only sixteen. I got him a job in the club then. I got him a job there as a waiter and to clean the smoke room. He knew I was gay. I think I found out he was gay after he joined the club. These things are very hard to explain. And yet they happen very easy. The staff hall porter ... he was gay too. We found out we were that way inclined, we'd had sex and he'd come to my room. Eventually it came out that this hall porter thought my nephew was very nice. I said, what do you mean? Oh, he said, yes, he came and stayed with me last night Well, I was shocked. I'll be honest! I was. And yet I was pleased in a way, you know. In fact his mother, my sister, Susan, was a lesbian for fifteen years too! She left Peter's father. She's quite open about it. Of course, she's remarried now. Quite well. Her husband now knows. He knows Peter's gay, he knows I'm gay.

There is only one senior officer who is gay at the club that I know of. I know Peter went home with him several times. It was through Peter that he found out I was gay. He come down to me quite confidentially, quite nice about it. Hello, Gerald, he said, you're a naughty boy like me, aren't you? Just in those few words. Well, I got the answer. I said, well, fair enough. We shook hands. If you're genuine, you've got to be genuine, it just comes and goes. You don't split on anybody. We had a fabulous time. We had a threesome once. See, you just take things as they come. See, you don't go looking for these things. Three of you in one bed, you have a bloody good night. Next night probably there's two of you, perhaps he's with somebody else and you're with somebody else. But once a week was ample for me. If you want enjoyment, it's no good going two or three times a week because where are you going to get the enjoyment out of it? The ecstasy's gone, isn't it? You've got to have a constitution like a stallion to be that way inclined. See, have things in moderation, just take things easy. And enjoy it when it's there.

You could tell those that were passive and who was active, or bitch and butch, put it that way. In nine cases out of ten you could always tell the butch from the bitch. If you get a bitch she'll put her hand down your fly, to find out what you've got. But if you get a butch, he'll put his arm round your neck, you know, as much as to say, come on darling, then his hand will slide down your back and down to your bum. Of course, now, you get some people come into the clubs who are only in there just to see what's going on. They are the class of person which I call bisexual. They want to, and yet they're afraid to. They don't know which way to move. You can always tell those people because they're so damned awkward. So there's no actual movement, you know. They come and they—there's no movement of the hand. It's all done with the word of mouth. You all right darling? Do you want to come home with me? You know. Well, in the gay world you don't ask a person to come home with you. Well, you always go by the movement of the hand.

I've never wanted another relationship since Phil, I'm an individualist, now. I got let down with that woman and then with Phil. When we split up, after I found that his affection had gone to somebody else, it hit me again same as the one on the feminine side. So I thought to myself, well that's it. No more. I'll keep myself to myself. If I want anybody I'll go good enough. Occasionally, yes. Actually I met one chap in the cinema. The Biograph. Years ago that used to be a hell of a place. Used to be fab. I've seen some things going on at the Biograph. Sitting next to each other and carrying on just as if they was in bed. Yes. Some with their trousers half down, laying on top of each other. And nobody saying a word. It used to be 25p when I went in there. It's gone up to 60p now—60p for the front stalls, 70p for the back.

I definitely think things have changed for the better. I say, look at the prostitutes. What did they do? They took them off the streets. So they've gone underground. They've expanded, haven't they? Same as homosexuals. But I like men to be men.

I don't like drag. I like to see Danny la Rue from the entertainment side of it. It's a real good act. But the drag bit, no. I wouldn't entertain it. To be honest I detest it. I don't think it's natural. If you're homosexual you're homosexual. I mean you don't want to throw it to the world, let them know you are homosexual. I'm homosexual now and to be honest I'm proud of it as far as that goes. 'Cos I use my homosexual life in a clean and sensible and a reasonable way. I don't flounce myself, this, that and the other. I'm not going to dress myself up to let somebody know I'm a bitch. Although I'm butch, but I can be bitch if I want, within reason. But, you know, I'm only talking in the past tense. See? That's as far as I can go.

2 A rough life

Fred was born in Barry, Wales, in 1894, into a family with eleven other children. The family was very poor and this was exacerbated when Fred's mother died and the children were deserted by their father. Fred was also an epileptic.

Fred had a number of jobs, including time spent in the army during the First World War. Most of his working life was spent on the railways, alongside of which he bred pigs and cultivated some land.

He had a successful marriage that continued throughout his adult life. Indeed he was devastated when his wife, his lifetime partner, died.

His homosexual experiences were all covert. When a gay liberation group started up locally in the early 1970s he began attending their meetings. He was then approaching his eighties. As by far the oldest member of the group, he became its mascot, and was given strong, solid support by the members, especially when his wife died. In his last years he lived with his daughter, but kept in contact with his new gay friends until his death.

I was born on 18 August 1894 in Cadoxton, just down the bottom of the street and round the corner.

My father was a stonemason, he was a wonderful tradesman. But then, of course, the drink, he used to drink heavily. It was worse when the older ones were growing up. He used to come home and beat them and turn them all out, and well he used to do the same when I was born, you see.

When I was born, the people in the end of the block, they didn't have no children and they wanted to adopt me. My mother says, no, she says, I've bred eleven, and every one I can manage.

We never had luxuries. We younger ones were brought up on pigs' slick, that's the slick melted down and made lard of, and the older ones used to have the butter. We younger ones used to have the pigs' slick on our bread, and fried bread and two eggs with a cup of milk made into scrambled eggs between three of us before we went to school. And, of course, we always had our own home-cured bacon.

Mother used to buy two little pigs and then she'd rear them to be porker size, and then she'd kill one and we children had to go out and get the orders to sell the joints of meat round to different people. She used the money that used to come in for that to feed the other one until he was about twenty score for bacon.

I remember once, now this is a laughable bit this! I remember once, when we killed the porker, I was sent out to get orders, and I went to the 'King Billy', as we used to call it, the King William Hotel in Cadoxton. I knew my father used to go there to drink and I thought, well I'll go there and they are sure to give me an order, which they did. It was two sisters running the pub, and I said, we're killing a pig, would you like to buy a joint of pork or a leg of pork? Oh yes, they said, we'll have a leg of pork and we'll have some of the spare rib, and we'll also have two dozen eggs. Oh, I ran home then, full of delight. So I went home and I told my mother about the order I had and she naturally thought it was wonderful. So I took the order, the pork and the eggs back to these two sisters that run the pub. When I handed it over the counter I naturally expected to get paid for it. But instead of getting paid for it, the one sister said to me, now, you go back and tell your father that's so much off the slate. Of course, I was almost afraid to go home. And the consequence was, when my father come home and learnt about it, he gave me a good thrashing for going there. Oh it was laughable!

I wasn't a healthy child. I had these fits to contend with, and they were terrible. They started when I was eleven years of age. One of my brother's horses run away with me, and that caused me to have fits. First of all, it started in school after this horse had run away with me. We were having singing lessons. There was a row of boys in front and I was standing on the chairs behind the boys, and I fell right across them, wallop. The teacher then had the boys to fetch me home, and from then on I had these epileptic fits. I had to avoid all excitement, and I had to avoid looking at any accidents. I was always very shy, and very nervous, as a boy and as a young man as a matter of fact, till I went in the army. If any of the older brothers had started to quarrel with me, I'd have a fit straightaway. These fits kept with me right throughout my life until after I got married. Of course, I told my wife and we got on very well together.

When I was thirteen my mother died. Within two years the home was broken up and we all separated - one went one way and another another. I never saw my father again till nearly four years after my mother died. I recognised him because he had one hand in his coat pocket. He always used to walk with his hand in his coat pocket. He taught us children never to put our hands in our trouser pockets. If you wanted to put your hand anywhere at all, you put the one hand in your coat pocket and then you've got the other hand free to walk with. And that's how I recognised my father. Well, as he come by, I says, hello father. Hello, he said, which one are you, he said, are you Fred or Peter? I said, I'm Fred. He came up to my sister's because I was lodging with my sister at that time, and he stayed there overnight. But my brother and I, we weren't willing for him to stay because he'd deserted us. I felt very, very bitter, you see. So, of course, he went on his way and that was the last I seen of him then till he was seventy and he become chargeable to the Board of Guardians, in Chepstow, and the Board of Guardians wrote to us to ask us what we were prepared to pay, subscribe so much a week, towards our father's keep. The seven, no, eight brothers (seven brothers of us really because one brother was an invalid from the Boer War) the seven of us, subscribed this money to the Board of Guardians.

My first job was tuppence an hour, when I was fourteen years of age. I worked for a man down the bottom of the street by the name of Harry. There was eight men and eight boys of us. We boys were the labourers, and we had tuppence an hour. And he'd give you one rise: you'd have tuppence ha'penny after you'd been there a twelve month. Well, when you asked him for the second rise, you see, he'd say, oh I don't know, now let me see,

I'm thinking about sacking half a dozen of you at the end of the week. So that stopped us from asking for any more. So, of course, I couldn't live on this tuppence ha'penny an hour. My brother, Peter, the one next older to me, he'd already gone to work for my brother-in-law at Tonyrefail and he wanted me to go there for companionship. He kept on and on, and so eventually I went there to my sister's to work for my brother-in-law. He was a master man taking on contracts with houses for slating and plastering.

I stayed there then for a year and nine months and when I asked him for a rise he said, oh, he said, you're not worth it, you're too small. Of course, my hat flew off then. I said, well I'm not stopping here to be made a slave of. Oh, he said, you won't get no more no matter where you go. Oh yes I will, I said. So I left him there and then, and I came back to Barry and I reported at the Labour Exchange. They sent me to Ranks' Mill where I earned sixpence ha'penny an hour straightaway, for hod carrying.

This was before the First World War. You see, in those days if you went on the dole the Relieving Officer would want to know what you did with the dole money, and if you spent it on beer or cigarettes, they'd stop me. Oh life was very, very difficult in those days.

My homosexual inclinations started when I was a boy of about fourteen. I didn't understand it then you see, but, of course, I was a lonely boy, and I never had the love and affection of a father, and my brothers weren't close together. The ones that would have loved me, and liked me, they were away working. But I used to look at older men and I used to sort of be attracted to them. And I've been reaching out all my life to put my arms around another man. And it happened when I got into the gay group. It's a wonderful feeling. And the affection that you get from another person of your own sex when you genuinely love one another, and they like you and you like them, not for sex, but for love and affection, it's wonderful. But when people are put in prison because they are homosexuals and they have sex with one another, then it makes you think another way, you see.

In my young days, in my boyhood days, of course, we used to

talk about sex with one another. It used to crop up then, same as it does now. We used to call it shagging one another, though. And if it was plain speaking, it was effing one another, you see. But it was usually shagging, you know, a boy shagged another boy or a man shagged a boy you see, but I didn't hear the word 'homosexual' till I came out of the army, about twenty-five, I suppose. From then on it more or less stuck in my mind that that's what I was.

I first heard the word 'homosexual' in the gang. I mean men talk amongst themselves when they pick up a paper and find somebody has been had up for having sex with another man, and, of course, it was looked down on them, you see. But it was a known thing with seafarers, oh dear me, yes. When I was a little boy I was warned about sailors. Of course I didn't under-stand what they really meant. But they warned us younger ones never to talk to sailors. Oh yes, because this is a shipping area you see. And when I was a young fellow I was a shapely, fine-built young fellow and I used to hear all kinds of remarks. Of course, my job was bending down, seeing to the fishplates like this, and when you go along the row, on the dock row, you'd hear, 'Cor, what would I give to shag him'. Then somebody else'd come along, 'I'd give ten years of my life to have a go at him'. You'd hear all this conversation, and so I've always regarded myself as homosexual but I never did anything about it until recently, when I joined the CHE group.

I was called up during the First World War, yes. I got rejected first of all. The doctor wouldn't pass me on any account, because of my cardiac debility and subject to being nervous. But finally I was called up.

Oh, the first night in the army. Ah, well now, I grieved so much through my life, every day, and I'm not jesting, I'm not ashamed to own it. I used to cry about my mother. And then the first night in the billets I went to go to bed. I was amongst all strangers and I had a terrible job of meeting strangers, because I was so shy and bashful. This was in Porthcawl, in Mary Street.

I palled up with a Geoff and we went on the east coast to a place called Elvedon. We were short of water, and we had one bowl of water between twelve of us for bathing. Of course, a lot of the boys was 'lousy'. Geoff and I, we used to pinch the water and go out behind the gorse and bath. It wasn't little short gorse in them days, at least not on the east coast. It was like young trees, so nobody could see you bathing there unless they came right on you. Of course, we used to bath in our birthday suits and that's the first time that I felt the love and affection of a man.

It had never entered my mind before. I was always scared. But we used to cut our arms around one another and nothing happened for weeks and weeks till this particular day. We'd had our bath and were sunbathing and Geoff got a hard-on and he rolled over on top of me, and he started making love like that. Of course that's when it all started. And oh it was lovely. I'll never forget it. Never forget it

There was the time in the army when I came back to be discharged. I came back from Purbright to Cardiff. In Cardiff barracks it was all strange chaps and of course we knew what sex was then, as soldiers and sailors and seafarers. And one particular night I was in the hut there and this young chap came in drunk. We'd practically all gone to bed, and we had the light on and he was singing there and so he strips off in the nude, he did, and comes over to my bed and, of course, when he come over to my bed he had a hard-on, and he said, come on Fred bach, you've got to have this. So I clutched hold of the clothes, and thought to myself, I'll learn him a lesson, as he went to pull the clothes off. Hey, hang on a minute, I said, on one condition. He said, what's that? I said, that I shag you first. And of course his old boy went down just like that! And they all burst out laughing now, make him look a fool. He never tried it on after.

Of course I never went with a woman in my life, other than my own wife. Never courted another woman. Was too shy. As regards getting married, it was the last thing I ever thought of because, well, it was unnatural if you can understand. I was never drawn to the opposite sex. The reason I got married was through having typhoid fever. I was in lodgings and I was that ill, I nearly lost my life. I said to myself, well Fred, the best thing you can do is find a good partner and get married to have some-body to look after you, and sure enough, she was a good partner. I had known her all my life. How it started was she sent

me a card with red roses on, and of course I knew that red roses
is love, and we started from there.

Before we got married we had a proper understanding with
one another, my wife and I. I said to her, now look, Doll, if
we're going to get married I'll have low wages. Yes, I know all
about that, she said, well I can sew, she said. But I said, oh no,
you're not taking in no sewing. My poor old mother was a dressmaker, and she spent hours and hours away at the machine
when she should be pleasuring. So you're not taking in sewing.
But if you like to help me, if we do get married, with the pigs
and the poultry, all well and good. Well, we had a proper understanding. I said, now look, I'll give you the wages, whether I'm
working or whether I'm ill, and don't ever ask me for any more.
And I shall never ask you for a penny back. All right, she said,
and we never asked one another for a penny. Right up till the day
she died. And we never quarrelled over money. If I sold a bunch
of pigs and had a good price for them, I'd give her as much as
£40 and that's going back years ago. And she wouldn't waste it.
She'd spend it in the house. And we never had a lot of pleasure.
Well, we didn't have the money. You see, I had to keep pigs and
poultry to eke out the wages. As I say, we never had a lot of
pleasure out of life. We used to go to the whist and dance now
and again see. When Freda, our daughter, came along we used
to take her as well. I'm blessed with a wonderful daughter, and
son-in-law. If I travelled all Wales I couldn't find a better one.
He's a hard worker and honest, and he's a real kind chap. He
very often catches hold of my hand and takes me across the
road. Sometimes he says, I don't know, pop, he says, I hope that
people don't think me and you are pansies!

In them days it was at least three years if you were caught
going with another man. You had to forget all about it, you see.
There was a chap in my life, Alex, not at that stage but after. He
was one of the locals and he used to go to sea. I knew him well.
He got into trouble, he had sex with a boy. He had come home
from sea unexpected and his wife wasn't home. He went to the
boozer and he gets pretty well drunk I suppose, and he went
through the park and the boys stared mucking about with him.
He took one of these boys back to the docks and had sex with

the boy and got put away for three years. So when he, Alex, come out of gaol he came to see me.

I was still as friendly with him, but not for sex, and I advised him not to give up the sea, to still go to sea because if he had a job ashore he'd always have someone poking their finger at him, you see. So the consequence was Alex went back to sea and I used to see him about twice or three times a year. He used to come and see me but there was never any mention of sex. Of course, he had a wife alive but he didn't have any children.

My wife never really suspected, though she nearly caught me out once. I was on the 'phone to Alex from Cardiff, and I was talking to Alex and she came along the passage, opened the door, and said, who are you talking to? Oh, a chap wanting to know about some timber I said, and I put the receiver down, and Alex understood, because we'd made the arrangement, that if I talked about timber or anything he'd know that somebody was about.

I've always preferred a male's company to a female's company and I do now today. I'd rather cuddle a man than I would a woman. Females never meant anything to me really, although I kept my vows, I was honest and I never went with another woman in my life other than my wife. But as regards sex with another man, well, I must openly confess that I wouldn't do it with every Tom, Dick and Harry. I have had sex with other men and still do if it comes my way and we agree, one with the other. I find a male's company is wonderful. There's something about your own sex. You're free and easy to talk and to give and to love. You're not bound to have sex, it's enough to love a person.

I used to keep the boar pigs, and I remember the first time I had it with a young farm labourer. He was eighteen and I was about twenty-six then. He brought the sow to the door and ... have you ever seen a boar serving a sow? Well, it takes about half-an-hour, and this particular time now, the boar was serving the sow in the pen like, and this young farmer kiddie says to me, hey, he says, don't you ever feel like a bit of sex when you see this going on? Aye, I says, how about it? Just like that. I didn't think no more. Oh, he says, I will if you will. And of course that did it. I was ready and he was ready. But I think that to love and

to be loved is the foundation of a happy life. I can prove that.
You could love a chap without having sex with him, you see.

About ten years back, there was a chap had up for impor-
tuning. I didn't know him from Adam, but I phoned him. He
had been fined £15. And at that time I had plenty of work, I
could afford to pay the proper rate of pay and I was always glad
of a bit of help with the garden and that. So I got to know his
phone number and I phoned him up and I said, don't be
alarmed, I'm not a policeman, I'm a gay man myself, and he fell
for it straight away.

What happened was his proper pal hadn't turned up when he
went to the pub to meet him. So he had a few drinks more than
he should have done and, of course, he goes to the toilet and
there was this young fellow there that he fancied, but he didn't
know that there were two of them and this one was a policeman
in plainclothes, see. They nabbed him straight away. And that's
how he had been fine £15. I went to see this chap and I had sex
with him. He was what they call impotent: he couldn't have sex
with you. So I had him for about three years. He had a bedsit
and I used to go up when his landlady was away. She used to be
away for about three months at a time. When she came back
home he used to come down here and I used to give him a job
to do, and we managed to do it outside in one of the outhouses.
But, of course, my wife never knew anything about it, see.

After this chap went off to London, I had another man then.
I used to see this chap when he was working, but I never knew
he was homosexual until I saw his name in the paper. I thought,
blimey, I never thought Johnny would do such things. He had
been sent down for three months, so I knew very well he'd have
a month's remission and, after the two months was up, I went to
see him at his address where he was lodging. They were very
discreet about it when I asked about him. They said, oh he's
away working at the moment, we're expecting him home any
time. Of course, he hadn't come home from prison yet. Oh well,
all right, I says, I'll call again, I'll come around in about a week's
time, so I did. When I went in a week's time Johnny was home.
Hello Johnny, I said, tell you what I've come about, I've got a bit
of work that wants doing. I want a bit of help in the garden and

that. Oh all right, he said, I'll be glad of a bit of a job. So he was to come the next day. Of course, he didn't know that I was homosexual, gay.

I took him into the shed. Before I tell you anything about work, I said, I want to tell you what I am and who I am. What do you mean? he said. Well, I said, I'm exactly the same as you, Johnny, I'm homosexual. And he nearly fell backwards, he says, never. Come on then, he says, how about it? Straight away. No, I says, I'm not ready for you now, I said. You come tomorrow, I said, I'll fix things up for you. So I had him back and, well, he used to come and work here until he got a job. I helped him over the stile, and put him on his feet until he got a job, and he was with me for two years coming back and forth.

The silly sod went and got himself into trouble again with boys. Two boys this time, on Barry Island. So when he came out of gaol, you know, this next time, I went to him and I said, now look Johnny, the best thing you can do is to clear out of this place altogether, I says. Because if you don't, you'll be in and out of gaol all the time. So Johnny took my tip and he went. Where he went I don't know.

I found GLF [Gay Liberation Front] because it was advertised. I phoned in and went in. I was nervous to a point when I first went in. I was coming up to eighty years old! And, of course, I've become one of the old contemptibles, one of the regulars, aye.

It's a pleasurable thing to belong to. To me, it's like going to church. I go into the meeting and sometimes I never have a kiss from anyone. But there is one man, the first thing he'd do when he'd come in and see me, he'd straight away cross the room, and we've never had sex with one another, and kiss me. He's from Newport, and he's always been fond of me. I went to a disco once and, well, I felt a bit embarrassed really, but I was dancing with a chap on the disco, like. They accept me. They don't mind about the age difference and it's really wonderful.

When I was married I never thought I'd meet gay people. I was hoping and praying that some day I would be able to mix in with gay people. Oh yes, and it's been one of the happier times of my life since.

When they put it in the papers first of all, I didn't approve of their correspondence. You couldn't hand that on to somebody else to read. They'd call a spade a spade you know, right out in the open. It was disgusting, some of the literature. I didn't hold with that. But you can talk in your own language and get to understand one another, and know what you're talking about without causing offence to somebody else, you see. The nagging part about it is I had to tell lies to my wife, you see. I used to make up tales. I'd go into Cardiff about once a week, maybe once a fortnight, once a month. And she used to think I used to go to the pub. I've never been in there in my life for a drink! And she'd say, well who did you meet tonight, Fred? Oh so and so. Mind I used to mention first names, you see, say John or Geoff or Mike. My wife would never have understood. It would have broke her heart.

We've had some lovely chaps come to the gay group, but we don't hold them you see, they go. Of course, the regulars, what we call the regulars, well I suppose I'm one of the regulars, they always come along. Very nice people. That's what I say, there's some lovely people in the world. It's only a matter of bringing them together, isn't it?

They were very kind, after my wife died. They did more for me than one of my brothers, he never even sent me a letter of condolence. But the group, they sent me a lovely letter of condolence. Which I thought was very nice of them. And my friend John, he came to the funeral. Of course, John was the only one that Doll ever knew, and she didn't know him until she got took to hospital. He used to visit her twice every day.

I didn't think they'd ever get to pass the change in the law about homosexuality, somehow. But I'm more than pleased that they have. It changed my attitude very much. You feel more free. It's a wonderful feeling. I'm hoping to have a chat with our minister because if it crops up I'm going to explain it to him. Now the Gay Christian Movement, I think that's going to be wonderful because they are very open about it. And openly admit that it's natural, which it is, natural.

I mean, for example, what's the difference between a homo-sexual, an alcoholic, or a gambling man? Which is the worst of those three? Not homosexuals. Oh no. There's love and affection with a homosexual. But with a gambling man, he don't trouble except for himself. And the same with an alcoholic. Some of them are disgusting. You can go into Cardiff and see the poor souls. I often thank the Lord that I'm not one of those. You follow what I mean? I think if Mary Whitehouse was to come to our meetings and see the way we are, she'd change her mind.

I did put a piece in the paper many years ago. I explained that since I've been going to the gay meetings, the people I am associating with now have given me back twenty years of my life. Signed, Old Fred. Name and address supplied if wanted. Well they printed that.

I go to church Sunday evenings. Then Monday I go to the whist, in the YMCA. Then Tuesday now I go to the whist in the hotel in Barry in the main street. That's what we call a partner drive, we have the same partner right throughout the night. Then Wednesday I keep clear in case someone wants to come and see me. Well then Thursday now, I go to the pensioners in the afternoon. And then Thursday nights I go to the Thursday night whist, in the Pioneer Hall. Friday afternoon I go up to the pensioners hall and we have a little game of whist there amongst ourselves - very often I'm the only man among the whole lot of women. Of course, they pull my leg, mercilessly. But I take it all in good part, and that's why they call me Fearless Fred! Friday night I go to the whist again. Then Saturday, I go to the whist in St John's. And that concludes the week.

I don't go to that gay meeting every Monday night. My whist players they want to know terribly where I get to on Monday night when I go to the gay group! They say, I would like to know where old Fred gets to on Monday night. He's got a girlfriend somewhere! I never lets on, I laughs; takes it all in good stride.

I expect you've come across, especially in London, some of these chaps that paint themselves up; well they're advertising themselves aren't they? I don't like that. I like a chap that shows himself by his actions. A lot of young people don't bother with those older people just because they're old. Well that's the people I like to be with. I could be lonely if I didn't find my own comfort. There's the point isn't it, I go out and amongst people, and I enjoy their company. And they enjoy my company too.

But, of course, unless they ask me outright, am I gay, I shall never tell them.

I've had a rough life, and I've had my lonely days in my young days, but I'm not lonely now. I've got all my friends, my gay friends, and if ever I do slip down and feel a little bit down in the dumps, I turns to one of my friends or they turn to me and it really bucks you up.

I haven't got a regular boyfriend now. But I'm still hoping. Oh yes. And I do have sex now and again. Oh yes. And I really believe that we gay people must love one another. It doesn't matter who we are or what we are, because we are all the same.

3 A loner's life

Norman was born in 1895 in Yorkshire, an illegitimate child brought up in his early years by foster parents. He then returned to his natural family, ostensibly to be looked after by his 'aunt' and 'uncle'. He discovered later, when applying for his birth certificate, that his 'aunt' was really his mother. He never revealed that he knew the truth, and maintained the fiction all his life, even with his closest 'cousin', in actuality his half-sister.

In this interview, conducted, in part, in the West London retirement home where he lived for the last years of his life, he talks largely about the first part of his life, up until the Second World War, and the rather nomadic existence as a journalist he then followed. Later, he worked in London for a news agency, until his retirement. In the retirement home Norman developed a close and touching relationship with a fellow resident, Patrick, a few years older than Norman, a heterosexual who had been married for over thirty years. Norman called Patrick 'daddy', as his wife had called him earlier. 'Fancy', Norman said after the recording ended, 'being in love with a man of eighty-five. Why does he want me?' All his life, as the interview reveals, Norman wanted an ordinary' or 'normal' man to want him. In his last years he found one.

I had an ugly childhood, and I was born in an ugly town called Brighouse in the West Riding of Yorkshire. My grandfather, this is the truth I'm telling you now, my grandfather had a small cotton mill in the town. My mother had been seduced when she was about twenty-one, so I suppose my grandfather, who would be a puritan, said, oh well, we must get rid of it. So I was farmed out to these Welsh people in Manchester, where I first realised I was a little boy. And I was a little boy in a house with an elderly drunken barber, Welsh, and his meek wife and their daughter Lucy. The barber's shop was in the house too. And, of course, I was a very withdrawn child, completely quiet.

I slept with my foster parents. They must have had sex one night I was there, sleeping, because I heard the mother say, 'not in front of the child'. I can remember this, yet at the time I didn't how what it was.

When I was about seven-and-a-half, the old mother died, and so there was the question of what to do with me. So they took me back to my Yorkshire relatives. There was a great hubbub. In the end I was taken to my own natural mother who in the meantime had married. She married a farmer who was also the manager of a shop and they had one little daughter who was really my half-sister. I had to call him my 'uncle' and my mother 'aunt' and my half-sister was my 'cousin'. So the next part of my life I really lived a lie, you see. It worked out that my mother, my proper mother, treated me badly, and my 'uncle' also beat me, not a lot but for me it was quite enough. I discovered my 'aunt' was my natural mother when I applied for a birth certificate, when I was eighteen. My family never knew I knew.

There was one episode that I had in this street where I lived. There were pubs and shops. I must have been sitting in the entrance to a pub and there was a little girl, and she wanted me to expose myself. I was shocked I was. Of course, I never told anybody. I didn't dare.

I was taken to school when I was very young. I adored school. All the schools I went to were ordinary boarding schools. I was very fond of a teacher, he must have been Welsh, called Davies. In those days they wore black suits. I can remember him in a black suit. I remember I liked him, and he used to cane me and then he used to say, oh I'm sorry. I shall never forget that. I talked a lot so I was always getting caned. I would walk along the street home, and I would be thinking about him. I wouldn't have words, I'd only have thoughts. And they'd be very, very, very pure at that point. Angelic. It was a pure affection: up here in my mind, not there in the crotch.

There was no masturbation in school or anything. But I knew

about it, I'll tell you why. When I was young, about, we'll say, eleven or twelve or somewhere around there, I had to sleep with Harold, a cousin of mine, who must have been about seventeen. Of course, he got me masturbating him, which I found very boring. I always remember that. I didn't see it as sinful. It was merely that he wanted to be masturbated. Of course, we didn't use the word 'masturbation'. One didn't know the words.

I didn't think of it as homosexual. I already knew about sex when I was very young. I knew there was something between men and women, that was the way I thought of it. I didn't know what homosexuality was. How should I know? In those days, I'm speaking of the beginning of the century, they never spoke about it.

I found out about men and women from books that came out, sort of 'what a young man should know'. I would look into these bloody books and, oh, they made me squeamish! The real thing that it shows is the complete lack of communication. And that's why now I'm mad on communication. The greatest priority: communication.

I ran away twice when I was young. The second time I must have been about sixteen. I ran away to London and I got caught in the train at Willesden, and they actually took me to Brixton prison for a night. Fortunately I've forgotten it completely. I only remember riding through London in the black van and looking out in the sunshine. I wasn't unhappy. My parents were a bit upset.

I lived in what you call the lower-middle class, not working class. Although I was a shop assistant when I started work, it was the lower-middle-class atmosphere. Children tended not to mix with other children from other streets, so you rather kept alone. When I was at school, although I'm a very friendly person, I never mixed with other boys.

I stayed with my own relatives till I was about eighteen, working in various shops. I worked in clothing shops, starting as an errand boy. I got five bob a week. It was all men, of course. There were no women employed then.

Finally I got a job at Rochdale, filthy Rochdale in Lancashire. And then the First War had come, so I applied for a job in

London. Of course, now men were leaving jobs, so I got a job in a shop in Upper Norwood near Crystal Palace. I was nineteen. Of course the point was that I never really, although so unhappy, never broke off my connection with my home and my real mother. It's the flesh and blood thing.

The first person I became friendly with, it must have been in 1915, I met at a theatre. His name was David, son of a doctor. He was living with his aunt, at Bexhill. I think he must have been a homosexual, he never married. But we never spoke about that. I knew Edward Carpenter through him. We never spoke about anything except theatres and books. I think he and his aunt had probably been to a lecture by Carpenter or something like that, you see. Complete lack of communication.

I had read *The Intermediate Sex* by Edward Carpenter, by this time. I was also reading Compton McKenzie, D. H. Lawrence, Dostoevsky, and my God, I was up there in the clouds, more brain than balls. I never read these new books about homosexuality now, I read Carpenter at that time. These recent books that you see in the papers I've never read. I like reading personal books. I read *Love's Coming of Age* and *Towards Democracy*. I had a copy when I was a soldier.

I saw Carpenter twice. Once in London, when he was staying in a boarding house in Tavistock Square. I can remember going there. I must have liked the old man, because when I went north, for a time I thought I would go and see him again. Of course, I didn't know that he was homosexual. I didn't even think of that. He lived with George Merrill, who naturally I wasn't interested in. I thought he was the gardener. It was in the garden that Merrill kissed me. I must have been only twenty-one. Not good looking. I was rather shocked, owing to my loveless early life. I didn't know anything about kissing. Fancy missing all those years. What a waste. I'd never been kissed. I don't suppose I showed anything, because I was a very polite young man at that time. Of course, when I read about E. M. Forster having his bottom pinched by Merrill I realised it was the same man.

Then came 1916 when they had conscription, and I was very glad, because, I thought, I'll get out of this stinking job. I was conscripted at, I think it was, eighteen. I have a picture of myself as a soldier, rather an ugly poor little soldier, looking very pathetic. I was completely withdrawn.

In the army too I made only one friend. A little chap called Walter. There was nothing between us. I was quite innocent. We never talked about anything. I can't remember any talk about homosexuality during that army period, around 1916. The men would swear a lot, but I didn't hear any talk, surprisingly. There were French brothels and I think some men went to them, but, of course, I never got near those sort of places.

You mustn't forget, the whole of those years was loveless. It's very odd, I read books about love but, of course, I didn't realise I ought to know about this. In the army I was very popular because I could talk. I knew a few French words and the officers liked someone with a bit of common sense.

In France, it was very primitive; all the soldiers were working-class men. A former barber, a former waiter, I got on very well with all of them. I got very friendly with a boy called David and I slept with him, because we had two blankets each, so we'd have one underneath and three on top. Of course, nothing happened. I mean I didn't want to sleep with him, but in the army they didn't bother about people sleeping together. It wasn't suspicious. People didn't even joke about homosexuality. I didn't realise I was homosexual. There were all these men and I saw them bathing and everything, but I was much more mental then, than sensual, and I think that's probably why I wasn't interested.

Towards the end of my period in the army I was in a convalescent camp in Croydon. It was there that I began to realise I was homosexual. I met this boy. He was this typical young English boy that I really like very much, an Anglo-Saxon type. I didn't even bother about his name. But, of course, I realise now I would push up to be next to him. I was very unselfconscious. I didn't realise what I was doing. I'm the instinctual type, you see. He must have realised. He did kiss me although there was no sex.

Then I get out of the army, deserted actually. Some friends helped me and I went to Ireland. Oh, I must tell you that whilst

I was in Ireland I suddenly became very good-looking. I suddenly blossomed out. But you mustn't forget my life was filled with other things at this time. I was not fanatically for boys then. I was a very late developer.

I was in Belfast, and then I became a shop assistant again. Wherever I go they have wars there. I used to mix a lot with all the radicals, so I was always with young men. I liked being with young men, but I didn't think of it in that way.

I did exactly like E.M. Forster: I fell in love with a tramway conductor. He was married too and I got him to send his wife away for the weekend, and I slept with him. Of course, he was quite a normal boy. Roman Catholic too. That was the very first time I had slept with anyone I wanted to sleep with, although we didn't have sex. I realised that this sleeping is not really what I wanted. Robert his name was. He was very nice about it. I've taken the greatest risks that one does in a life.

I tried to cuddle with him but I'm frightfully sensitive, and he didn't want it, and didn't want to say he didn't want it. I'm not one of the talking type when I'm with young men. I just love them. I kept up with him and we had quite a nice friendship.

Then I went back to London. Even now I wasn't desperate for young men, but I went a great deal to the ballet and I went to the Empire at that time in Leicester Square. I was standing in the circle and there were some young men there. I saw someone, and I went up and picked him up. It was rather funny, because I used to share him with Siegfried Sassoon. He wasn't a policeman, but he was big like a policeman. Sassoon used to put his arms round Roger. Of course, I was rather jealous. I was frightfully intense with Roger. But he wrote me a letter once, and he said, I remember the sentence, I am not a homosexual. Well, of course, I knew that. I never slept with him. But I knew him all my life. He married, you see. I went to Calcutta, and when I returned to London I noticed that Roger had become rather cold. But I realise now what had happened. He'd met his future wife. She was a Cricklewood sort of type. He was a very good man was Roger.

I was in London for a while, then I went to India, as a freelance journalist for the *Telegraph*. In India I had a little tiny episode with an American who wanted me. I discovered quite early I didn't want to be wanted, I was the one who wanted to want, to be the lover, not the beloved. I discovered that, so, of course, I had to say no. I didn't want anyone if they fell in love with me. It's because I have this desire to want. I thought it was impossible to have a mutual relationship where you loved each other.

That was the one affair I had. Then I got to know two very nice young Indians. I slept with one. It was quite all right. I played with him. The Indians are very sexy. But in India I didn't have anything really exciting. You see I hadn't forgotten Roger. Another thing that is very strong in me is fidelity. Promiscuity too, but also fidelity. They're both very strong in me indeed, so I was always thinking of Roger. Then I came back, in the summer of 1921, to London.

This was where I picked up a boy called Herbert, at Speakers' Corner. He lived with his father in the Borough. No mother. So we never met in a room. We wanted to go to Belgium. When I think back I often think, good God, why did he allow me to take him? But I went with him. We both paid our own fare, although it was very cheap then. I slept with him. Of course, there again it was quite hopeless because he didn't want anything. I understood. The trouble is I was discovering very quickly that everyone admired me for my mind and not for anything else.

I told him, I don't like your name, Bert. You're going to be Michael. I'd read about Michael in Compton McKenzie. And he got the name Michael. He had it legalised. He married a girl later. And I went and stayed with them in America. He then worked for one of the big trade unions. He died in *The Times* as Michael. I was once looking at *The Times* and there was my Michael, my created Michael. He was my age. He liked me very much. We saw a lot of each other. He was very good-looking, of course. This English type. He was the type I like very much. But there was nothing more to it. We never spoke about it. Mustn't forget these people, Roger and Michael. After all those things, we never spoke about it. But we kept in touch, because we were all readers and we were all radical.

Still in this summer of 1921, I went over to see James Joyce in Paris, from Belgium. I went over to Brussels and then over to Paris. I was getting rather desperate, because I was working at Whiteleys department store for twenty-five bob a week, this was 1921. I will admit they gave you meals. Trouble is, I've never made use of people, I'm not the pushy type. Although Roger was a journalist then, none of them helped me. Friends kept on saying to me, you should be a journalist. But what was the good, I didn't know how or what. I was quite desperate.

That summer a friend told me about someone living in Prague on nothing as a painter. Being from Yorkshire I said, of course, nobody could live on nothing. So I said I will go to Prague. I was still working at Whiteleys. I booked my journey to Prague and then I had £10 spare. I didn't know what I was going to do. I wasn't frightened. I'm not physically brave, but I have other kinds of courage.

I went about the end of October, beginning of November. All these people came to see me off at Victoria, most of them didn't know each other. This was still 1921. So all these countries were not in a very good state. I went through Germany, and I got to Prague. There was a couple there, Edwin Muir, the poet, and his wife, very poor. In fact, they asked me if I had any money and I told them I'd got £10, that's all I'd got. But they helped me. They found me a room and they took me to a restaurant and told me what the food was. In about two days I got a job in the Cunard Line and very soon after I got a job in a school teaching English. I was very lucky.

I had no sexual experiences. They're not homosexual in that way in Prague. I did have two emotional adventures, Alexander, this very heavy Scotsman from Aberdeen University, and Vladimir, the grandson of a poet. I was quite satisfied going about with all the people. I had a very lively time dancing and all this is kind of thing. There was one white Russian I liked very much and he went to Berlin. He said, you should go because in Berlin there were many homosexual places.

I stayed from the end of '21 till mid 1923. I wanted to go to Russia, but it was too difficult. So I went to America instead. Yes. But before, ha, I'd forgotten, before I went to America, in '22, I went on tour of Europe for two months, July and August.

I did it on £40. Hotels, railway journeys, newspapers, theatres, every bloody thing. And I had one very nice adventure. I was picked up in Munich by a beautiful Italian. And I was terrified of him. I thought, what will he do to me? you know. He rather looked the Valentino type. Well anyway, he picked me up in the front of the railway station. And I lived in a hotel near there. And fortunately he was in the same street. So he took me to his hotel. Very enormous bed. And he must have realised that I was very unhappy. So nothing happened. You see I thought he would want sex, and that was the one thing I wasn't going to do. I really felt very adamant about this. You see, those were the years when I was growing up. I was a slow developer.

I had a lovely time on the boat to America, with young men galore. I learnt by now that I could seduce young men. I don't mean physically, but get them. I finally got a very nice Swiss boy when leaving the boat in New York. We slept in a hotel, not together, in different beds, nothing happened, I didn't want anything. Then I got a room in New York. I knew no one in America and I had to get a job. It was boiling hot, so that I wasn't thinking about sex. Then I went to peddle encyclopedias in a small town, up in the north of New York State, in the country. I met this very nice boy, Sam. I really played it quick there. I met him at a door selling medical books. So I talked to him. He didn't know I was admiring him. I said, oh well, what about taking a room? So we got a double room. And I made my advances. Very innocent. Of course he didn't want anything. It was a flop. But I didn't mind. He didn't throw me out of the bed.

When I saw him I liked him because I liked his face. I'm always attracted to their faces, not their pricks. He could have been rough and thrown me out on the floor, but he didn't. It reminds me of an adventure I had some time later, travelling from America to Europe. I met a very nice young Pole, so I thought all right, I'm going to sleep with him. I'm afraid I had become very cynical. I started thinking about the sleeping before it happened. So we got to Paris. I think he was on the way to Warsaw and I was on the way somewhere. I took him to a hotel. When I was cuddling him he said, I let you do this, because you are an artist. I realised they all saw it as something different, not for what it was. I always fell in love with people who weren't homosexual. I went to Boston, Massachusetts, where fortunately I got a job exactly opposite Harvard University. Lovely. Hundreds of young men. I was surrounded with young men. But I didn't sleep with anybody, except a young American who had a crush on me. I let him sleep with me once. Of course, I wasn't attracted to him at all. So I slept very coldly, and he made the remark I'll never forget, 'Why are you so cold to me?', Very sad. He lives in Madrid now. And he has a friend called Alfonso, whom I like very much. I like to keep in touch. I'm a faithful dog.

I hadn't knowingly met any other homosexuals at this point. In Boston I did meet one. But I only knew him through someone else, not personal experience. He was a professor at Harvard. I didn't meet one personally till I got to Vienna when I was twenty-nine or thirty. This was when I met real homosexuals and began to take a real interest in them. I said to myself, oh well these are all those public schoolboy homosexuals, and I felt rather superior. Anybody can be a homosexual at public school, I always said, I'm the real thing. With me I think I was born that way. It was very curious, the homosexuals I began to meet always seemed to me to be mummy's boys. I became very interested in analysing them.

I had a very hectic life in Vienna, that way. At least two or three times a week I would pick someone up. So easy. They were at all the pissoires or hanging about the railway station. All ordinary boys who wanted a bit of money. They weren't full-time prostitutes.

The prostitutes were at the Russian baths. I used to go to the baths with this old man. He loved picking them up. He was so ugly that, of course, he had little choice. They used to walk about with a sheet over them and then open it.

The boys on the street that I picked up were all gentle Austrian boys. They just wanted a bit of money. Harmless. I made no demands of them, so, of course, I kept on picking up people and couldn't do anything. I picked up a beautiful Bulgarian at the opera. I got to know him but I couldn't do anything. I had a bad habit of getting to know people who were of no use to me that way but it didn't irritate me because I liked them.

Vienna was the first city where I ever told a woman I was homosexual. Made her laugh a great deal, she called me Sheherazade because my stories went on and on and on! I told her about all these adventures, picking up the Russian, the Bulgarian, etc. I spent my time in Vienna and used to go to Prague once a week and pick up people in railway trains for money. So easy, because I had plenty of time. Vienna is where I started really being promiscuous. It's an easy place to be promiscuous and I'd already decided I would be. I had a terrific life there.

In New York and Prague I'd had very little experience of anything. So now I had all that. I had also started my real journalism, freelancing, and this promiscuous life went side by side with working very hard at my typewriter. I had a room in a flat, which must have cost about a shilling a day. I could take someone there. I used to take a young man there every week.

We are now back in the thirties; 1931, no '30. The depression had started. I went off to America. I stayed with friends in the southern states, in a country club. Right in the middle of beautiful scenery with oranges growing. That was the year my deserter story appeared in a magazine. They paid $250, which must have been about £50 or something. It wasn't very much.

But anyway I came back to Europe and then went back again to Florida, and then things had got rather bad; my old job had gone. So I went to work in a yacht club in New York. Well then, in 1932, things had got so bad in America I thought I'd better go. I'd been working on yachts. There's nothing more luxurious than yachts. You should see the yachts out there. But I lost the job. Everything was running down. So I went back to London. I just didn't know what to do. So I thought to myself, well I've never been to Moscow and finally I'll go.

I was not a communist. I was what you would call a fellow-traveller. I managed to get a visa. I'd written some articles about Pudovkin, the film producer, so I managed to go to Moscow by train. I've forgotten where I got the money from. An article about German writers for America I believe. I was always getting money by selling books or writing articles. Fortunately, I got a little job on the Moscow English evening paper. I got there just before the November parade—this was 1932. It got very cold and I stayed till about Christmas time. I had a young friend with whom I'd slept, but he was not homosexual.

I returned to London, just as Hitler came to power in Germany. I came from Moscow, Berlin to London. (Incidentally I met Isherwood in London. I met him in Berlin in 1931, and now I met him again. And I went to tea with him in Kensington.)

Well, then I went to a national newspaper to see if there was anything doing. They had just got rid of their pro-Hitler correspondents so they had nobody. They said, Will you go to Berlin for us? So I was sent in 1933, on a five guinea salary. I had about one suit, and one suitcase. Thank God I know German and could write journalism. I went to Danzig first to cover the election, then to Berlin. I remained there from about May '33 until August 1939.

They were putting homosexuals in prison at this time. But I still had an affair. My great adventure for that period was Wolfgang. He was a boy of twenty-one. I was thirty-eight. Old enough to be his father.

I met him one Sunday. I went to the American church and, as I was walking out, I saw him there. I just said this is it. Instinct. He was with a lady I knew and so I was introduced and I had him to lunch. He became my friend. I got him to come and live near me, across the road, so he could run in. I used to talk English, I refused to talk German with him. I used to take him to the movies and buy him food. I looked after him and I liked doing it. I would take him to tea parties. Being an attractive young man, women naturally tried to take him away. I told Wolf to tell them I looked after him, that we didn't belong to them.

Where I lived they always called me 'kind'. I said, don't call me kind. English people are kind, we don't want to be called kind every time.

When I slept with him I played about with him, of course. He was very good about kissing. He gave me lots of affection. Was very good that way. But he wasn't a homosexual. Oh no. The point is, I knew that some day he would marry, and, of course, one day he did. He married during the Second World War when I was away. I knew he was quite normal. As I've said, I have this kink about normal people, if you can call it a kink.

Alongside my relationship with Wolf, I used to visit a young man I had picked up. He lived in a slummy part of Berlin. And he had a wife and child. I used to visit him and we would go to bed in the next room, with his wife in the other room. I gave him money. After supper I would take a taxi to there, go to him and return to the office from there. I used to fit it in. I never told Wolf. I don't know what Wolf's attitude would have been. We never spoke about anything like that anyway. I didn't say, Wolf I love you and all that to him. I used to think everything in my head.

This is very interesting psychologically, because most people have the illusion that all homosexuals behave the same. It's ridiculous. I mean all homosexuals do not behave the same. And I'm quite sure a lot of normal people think that we're all fucking all the time. Absolutely ridiculous.

I came back to London in August 1939. During the war there were a lot of soldiers in London who wanted a night's kip. So, of course, it was quite easy to say, well come and sleep with me. I had a room in Marble Arch. I've been rather amused, because it's a great triumph to get people who are not a bit interested, to accept all this nonsense. I picked up a lovely boy in Hyde Park, a soldier, from Grimsby. I took him home and I began sucking him off. And you know what he said to me? I wouldn't let anyone else do this to me except you.

I was hit occasionally by people I had picked up. Once in New York in my room, once in Vienna and once in London. But not very much. I had a little adventure in 1940. I picked up some wonderful Canadians in Leicester Square, lounging against a pub and, when it opened, they all went in and I followed them. Sat next to them. I got to know one of them, a Canadian Mountie. I was living in a boarding house in Mecklenburg Square, and I took him home. He was a great drinker, so I was able to supply a bit of drink. He was very beautiful. But, my

God. It's a wonder he didn't kill me. I didn't do anything, of course.

Another time I went away down to Devon and Cornwall for a holiday. Rather stupidly I picked up someone and, although there was nothing to it, I took him to the hotel where I was staying. Well, this chap reported me, so when I got back to London, in my boarding house, Scotland Yard came to see me. I was terribly upset and he said, you've been reported as picking up soldiers in the park. I said, yes. I'm homosexual, I said. I tried to hide some pictures of Wolf. But, thank God, nothing happened. I was very worried about it. I didn't have any qualms about saying I was a homosexual. Of course he was just a big flat-foot. He said, what do you do? Well, I said, I don't do anything. I said, I just hold hands. Well, I mean, fancy asking you what you do.

There were many guardsmen around during this period. I didn't meet many, but I did meet a few. I didn't have any thoughts about it, except that they were very strong men and, of course, that was all right. It was easy to get guardsmen anywhere, wherever they happened to be hanging around. I don't smoke so I can't say, would you give me a light. So I would just go up and say what are you doing tonight? I'd make conversation, thank God I can talk. I found everybody very easy. Don't forget, if you can talk, you can nearly always conquer. That's the one great key to success.

It wasn't very expensive since no one had a lot of money. In wartime they wouldn't expect more than ten shillings. A pound was quite a lot. Wages didn't go up till about 1960. I never met any homosexual guardsmen. In any case, I would have been put off by that.

Everybody wanted money, of course. One didn't expect people to have it for love. No, no, because I never met homosexuals you see. They were also looking ..., but they weren't looking for me. Well, not that I knew of.

I haven't known many people who lived together. I couldn't do it. I'll tell you why. Because, you see, I would never live with another homosexual, so, of course, that is out for me, and poor things, I could never ask an ordinary person to live with me.

I've never felt guilty about anything. I'll tell you why. I belong to that world you read of in books sometimes, of very innocent people. No, I hadn't the slightest feeling of guilt. When I first knew, of course, the trouble was I thought I was the only one, you know what it's like in England. I only feel one thing. I'm sorry that it cuts me off from people, because I have this demand for people.

I've been a left-winger all my life. I believe in the planned society. But I didn't connect this with my homosexuality. I have very strong feelings about this; people won't accept you if you are known to be a homosexual, that's the feeling I have. I don't really care. But I do feel it's a pity that it does cut one off. I've always been liked, you see, but I do think if the whole of my life had been labelled as homosexual, I might not have been. I have told very few friends that I am homosexual.

I don't like the word 'queer'. I don't like 'gay'. Because queer and gay mean something else. Remember I'm a word man, and I object to them taking the word gay. I always would say I'm homosexual. I mean that is the proper word. I'm not queer. A lot of people are daft, fewer are queer.

I wasn't involved in the campaign to change the law in the 1960s. I never want to change the law. I like to change the government, not the laws. I vote against the Conservatives. I am a Labour supporter. Not, of course, that I support everything they do. I feel I'm for the Welfare State, but I do feel they made a mistake in trying to look after every single human being in the country. It can't be done. They will go bankrupt. I have benefited very much by the National Health Service. They must have spent hundreds of pounds on me. I once asked a doctor, why are you doing all this for me? I wouldn't have minded a beautiful doctor, of course.

I think the media gives a false idea about homosexuality. The media exaggerates everything, and a lot of people who watch television, and who go to the cinema and who go to theatres will get the idea that homosexuals are feminine and amusing. There's been too much publicity from my point of view. I shudder, I shudder. I sometimes read *Gay News*. I read that with quite an interest, but often it irritates me. I think too much is devoted to groups. I'm not very fond of groups. I think they're boring. I don't like groups of Boy Scouts and groups of Girl Guides.

Frankly, I haven't thought about the future. The only thing I would like is more tolerance. You can't ask for more, you see.

I've had no fantasies in my life at all. Later on in my life I thought that the ideal friend would be a wonderful English man. I don't mean like Prince Charles either. Also, when I was younger, I must have read it in a book, I used to have an idea that I would like to know somebody who was crippled and that I would wheel them you see, a young man, and I would wheel them in a wheelchair. I must have read this in a book and thought, oh how nice, but I wouldn't have been strong enough. But I don't dream very much. I'm very earthy. I think that's Yorkshire. To me there's the earth and this and everything, and it's all very clear. Everything is very clear for me.

From one point of view I rather regard myself as an arrested adolescent. Very often I feel quite young inside, and I very often think of myself as a young man, although I'm an old doddy. I'm quite sure that my emotions have remained at about the age of twenty-three. I don't think they've ever changed.

4 A respectable life

Gregory was born in 1897 of upper-middle-class parents. After a public school education he pursued a professional career as a consulting engineer, though he also sustained a continuing interest in the arts. He became a pillar of his local community, and chairman of a local charitable trust. Alongside this, however, he led an active homosexual life, living for most of it with a partner, a relationship that ended only with the partner's death. This relationship seems to have been fully accepted by the partner's family, and grudgingly acknowledged by Gregory's father.

In this interview, Gregory describes his life, effectively in two separate worlds: the private and the professional.

I was born in 1897. Very old now! I was the only son. I was never very close to my father. He was an extremely clever person. A great raconteur, he held a very important position in the government service. He rather despised me for being interested in art. He had no idea about architecture, or furniture or anything of that kind. He was a literary person, very well read indeed, but he thought it was feminine or something to be interested in the arts. Which is quite extraordinary. We have nothing whatever in common.

I was very devoted to my mother. She died first, then my father died, having married a woman I didn't like at all, quite soon after my mother's death. Anyway, when my father died he left her everything, and not a penny to me. Not one penny. Nor to his brother. Not even a book.

I think I always liked boys. I used to play about with other boys, always. I enjoyed having fun and games as it were with boys at school. And I used to go about with girls too. Not in the intimate sense at all. Although I liked girls, and I like women today, to talk to, they don't interest me sexually in the smallest degree, never have.

When I was at school, at Westminster, I was very friendly with a fellow who is now dead. I was ill at my parent's home. And he came to see me. And he said, do you know, I've found out something extraordinary? I met a fellow called Jack, you must meet this man, who was a few years older. And I think that is how it really started. Apart from goings on at school, I didn't know about the homosexual world at all. And it was my friend who told me about Jack, and he introduced me into that world, as it were. I must have been less than eighteen I should say. It must have been about 1915 or something, because I was still at school.

I knew that it was illegal. I knew that I'd have to be careful and that sort of thing. But I never felt guilty. Never. I feel that I'm made that way and therefore I don't feel any sense of guilt whatsoever. None at all.

I tried to get hold of any book that touched on the subject, yes. I still do. There were Leonard Green's books that came along. And later I got on to the remarkable book, *Mr Norris Changes Trains,* by Isherwood. I've just actually read *The Naked Civil Servant,* which I hadn't read before. I think he was a very stupid man. Absolutely ridiculous to go about advertising himself like that. In fact, some women friends have said how courageous they think he was. But I don't think of it as courage. I think it was sort of pigheadedness, really, to go about with hennaed hair.

I read Edward Carpenter's *The Intermediate Sex,* of course. And indeed I lent it to the parents of this friend of mine. And I think I probably have it still somewhere. Yes, I certainly read that, and I read, what was that doctor fellow's name? I can't remember, Havelock Ellis, I read his books. I've always been fortunate, at least the last two doctors I've had have been homosexuals. Which is always very convenient and nice.

I used to go to meetings of the BSSP [British Society for the

Study of Sex Psychology] in my early or mid-twenties. I think it was a monthly affair, and I met Edward Carpenter there. When I say I met him, I didn't have any conversation with him really, or very little. Many of the members were old men, at least they seemed to us old men.

By this time my mother had introduced me to a boy who was at my old school, thinking naturally that I would be interested. She knew the family very well. There were three boys and one girl and she brought the eldest boy to a flat in which I was then living in Westminster. He was very nice and I got to know the others and used to go there to tea, and I discovered that this eldest one was homosexual. He told me that one of his brothers was homosexual too and he wasn't quite sure about the third one. And also that his sister was very eccentric! Well, I got to know this eldest brother very well, and then I met his younger brother, who was exceptionally attractive, quite unbelievably so. Younger than me, and we started a relationship.

He used to confide in his sister, which was a great mistake. To cut a long story short, his sister told her husband, who was a solicitor and the solicitor went and told the parents. The elder brother, who knew all about my relationship with his younger brother, came and told me all this. We were staying then down in Dorset, on holiday. I said, well the only thing for me to do is to go and see your parents. I was very fond of them and they were very fond of me. I went down and I said, this is all perfectly true. And they said, we do understand! They were very understanding. And the father suggested that the best thing would be for this younger brother to live with me! Which he did, for many years. Whenever I went to any party or dinner in his parents' house with him I was treated like a sort of son-in-law. It's an amazing story.

They were very angry with the sister's husband. When the third boy was married I was invited to the wedding, naturally, and I met the bride, of course, whom I liked and also the brother-in-law was there and the sister. My friend's parents told the brother-in-law that he'd jolly well better be pleasant to me and make friends with me, which he did. And now, unhappily, the younger brother, who lived with me so long, is dead. The sister and the brother-in-law keep up with me. I get cards every Christmas, from them, with love, you know.

I told my father I was homosexual, who was horrified about it. I didn't tell my mother. I was perfectly willing to, but I didn't. He said it would be wiser not to. When my mother died, my friend's parents wanted their eldest boy to represent their family at the funeral. My father wouldn't have him. There was a fearful to-do over that, which was very distressing. Anyway, they were going to write a letter to my father deprecating his attitude. I persuaded them not to in the end. And I remained very friendly with them.

With my father, it was simply sort of masculine dislike of that sort of thing. I don't think my mother would have minded a bit. I don't know whether she knew or not, it was never mentioned, and she and I got on extremely well. And that's really the background of the whole thing.

I don't like clubs, I've never belonged to one. I don't go to bars, because I don't drink and I hate the atmosphere. I was never a constant visitor to queer pubs. I don't like them. I used to go to the galleries. And, of course, there were an awful lot of cottages and so on. Tremendous, in those days. But the police nowadays have more or less closed them all down, and I think they're so much more vigilant than they were. Strangely enough, since the law which has made it legal for two people inside a house to enjoy each other's company, the early sort of public meeting of homosexuals and so on seems to have disappeared, except in certain queer clubs.

I've never had anything to do with a male prostitute. Never. I never go in the West End and Piccadilly or anything like that. I suppose it has changed, I believe they hang about in Piccadilly Circus tube station an awful lot. I would never have anything to do with them, in any circumstances. I would much prefer, if I wanted something promiscuous as it were, to go to the Biograph cinema, where I think you get a better type of person probably. I did meet one. He had the nerve to say, why don't you take me out for a drink? And I said, what on earth should I take you out for a drink for? I haven't the slightest intention of doing so. I was rather unpleasant, but he had no right to ask me that, and I wasn't the least interested in him or anything.

I was paid once. And it was entirely embarrassing. I remember, it was years ago, I'm speaking of soon after the war ended, the Second World War. I was working at the Admiralty at the time. Working very hard. And I used to have to struggle back to my home at night. Anyway, one night this particular thing happened. There's a famous place behind a pub in Camberwell, which was very interesting. And there was an army captain there, who showed interest in me, and I in him. And he said, oh well, there are a lot of ditched houses over there, let's go round there. Which we did. And afterwards he pressed a ten-shilling note into my hands. I said, I don't want this money, I don't take money, I enjoyed your company, and so on. I said, I will not have it. He said, but you've got to have it. I said, I won't have it. And he went on and on. And eventually pressed it into my hand and ran. Now I think he got a thrill out of paying people. Most extraordinary.

I like people of all types. Frankly I have had working-class friends and non-working-class friends. Many of them. As I get older I probably get more attracted to working-class types I think. But one doesn't come across them very much now, and, of course, I have to be very guarded, being a consulting engineer. Many a time have I crawled underneath the basement of a house or something with a very nice looking engineer, but never have I had anything to do with any of them, never. I made that a rule.

I don't think you can say there are more homosexuals in any one class than another. I think it's a certain cross section right across the country. As far as I'm concerned age doesn't enter into the thing at all. I do admire some attractive-looking young men certainly. But that's purely artistic appreciation I think. I'd be very happy to go to bed with them probably. Strangely enough gerontophiles turn up. And it's a very good thing that that is so in life, absolutely!

I loathe the word gay, which is ridiculous because I think that homosexuals are not necessarily gay at all. Often serious-minded people. Certainly they can, as everyone else, be gay on occasions. And also, it's American. I object to American words being introduced into the British vocabulary. I never use it. I use the word homosexual if talking quite seriously about it. I've used the word queer for many, many years. And I've used 'so': he is 'so'. That was a general thing.

I do think that homosexuality is too widely discussed today. And that has aroused suspicions among people. Some people are still very anti despite the fact that there are so many plays and novels on the subject and so on and so forth. And I'm not the sort of person who would like to discuss it with people who are not that way inclined themselves or particularly interested in it. And I know lots of people with whom I'm extremely friendly who have no homosexual tendencies at all, as far as I'm aware.

I've found it easy to have two separate lives really. No problem at all. No. Anyway I'm careful not to mix the wrong people and that sort of thing, but I do on some occasions mix people. Of course, you would never suspect for a moment that they were homosexual. I mean they have so many other interests as well.

5 A teacher's life

David was born in 1904 and was taken almost immediately to China, where he spent his early years. His education was in England, first at boarding school and then at Oxford.

David's career began in the colonial service in Nigeria. He became quickly disillusioned after witnessing a murder trial that resulted in the execution of a sixteen-year-old boy. For the rest of this career David worked as a teacher in Germany, Jersey and England; except for a brief spell in the Guards.

His sexual experiences have been wide. From an early age he had experiences with other boys and then men. Whilst at Oxford he had a sexual relationship with a working-class woman from the town. He eventually married whilst he was in Jersey. It was during this period that David began to form paedophiliac relationships. After the discovery of one such relationship at the school he had taught at for twelve years, the headmaster asked him to resign. This was at the beginning of the 1950s. He subsequently separated from his wife and moved to the mainland, returning only for holidays. In his later life he taught English as a foreign language in London. He became involved first of all in Gay Liberation politics in the early 1970s, then in pro-paedophile groups. He died just as these became the subject of police investigation, shortly after the interview took place.

Well, I was born in 1904 and six months after my appearance I was taken to China. My father was building the Canton-Kowloon railway at that time. He was in a sense a successful man; he had a big job. Very well paid, especially in China. This was a semi-colonial situation really. He left school when he was fourteen, because his father wanted to send him into the railway workshops to acquire technical skills. It was, at that time, rather like going into the aircraft business, because at the end of the nineteenth century, the railways were the important thing. The railways were wanted all over the world, in Argentina, Africa, India, Asia. Any railway engineer worth his salt was able to hold down a big job. My father was a self-made man.

My mother, on the other hand, though not an aristocrat in any sense of the word, has a lineage that goes back to French Huguenot stock. All of which is quite interesting and has an effect upon a chap. For example, I can never forget that one of my ancestors was beaten to death by Papal Dragoons at the time of the Huguenot uprising.

Actually, my mother was brought up very simply in Australia. She never went to school because there weren't any schools, she was privately educated by a tutor, and she was also a brilliant musician.

I was brought up in China by a Chinese Ama, and I have a terrific pro-Chinese feeling. Mao Zedong is a great hero for me, not only for communist reasons, but in a national sense. Also, I have a feeling for China that is purely romantic. I find myself thinking, sometimes even saying, just wait until those thousand million Chinese get going. The Japanese can do what the Japanese have done, just wait for the Chinese, they'll show the world.

I did have one little sex experience, which I can remember, with the other children who lived in the compound. German children I think they were, because my father's engineers came from various parts of the world. There was a little community of engineers. I don't think that that sexual event was particularly important, but I just happen to remember it in the way that children do. It showed also my sexual life was beginning early, as I think it always does.

My parents, rightly or wrongly, had the idea that it was impossible for me to be educated in China. So my mother brought me and my sister home to England when I was seven and we were both put into this school that had the advantage of being a sort of repository - you could leave children there not only during the school term-time but during the holidays as well. It was a bit unique in one sense, as it was a co-educational school, one of the only ones at that time. In that sense it was modern. Also there were one or two modern ideas connected with it. We had a Swiss educationalist, who came over and lectured. I can remember this because I was so amused; he spoke in this slightly foreign way, and he said, to be a good teacher it is necessary to have a normal sexual life. The poor headmaster's wife, her jaw sort of dropped and she went pale. There had been no talk of sex, of course, I mean, you know, the most fearful thing in the world.

We used to have chapel twice a day, three times on Sunday. I happened to have, fortunately or unfortunately, a boy's voice and I sang the whole repertoire. I say, boasting, that I know the whole liturgy forwards and backwards and upside down. It left a terrific mark on me, I never really got over it until my old age. In fact, the whole middle part of my life was spoilt with this religious business. I became high church and converted to Rome. I was very young. I was only seven, and I can remember in this little kindergarten class taking out my penis and playing with it. The mistress saw this and she said, come here David. So I went. And she said, would you like to tell the headmaster? I burst into tears and said, oh no, and that was the beginning and the end of my sexual life in school.

I did have an encounter at the age of eleven with a nine-year-old boy. His father was in the Indian Civil Service and, because we both stayed in the school during the holidays, we were put in the same bedroom. Sexual things developed, but that was all, because normally you were in dormitories and it was much more difficult.

In our school the anti-sex business was so colossal that almost everything was successfully tabooed. On the only occasion a master did have sex with a boy, the boy promptly told the head boy who told the headmaster and that master was dismissed overnight. Nobody knew anything about it. It was all hushed up and we were just told that he had gone to enlist in the forces, during the war.

At that time I didn't regard myself as homosexual, I never thought of this word, nobody knew such a word. It was just something that you did. When I look back and think about my wasted youth, all the sex that you might have had and didn't have, it really wasn't true. This reminds me of Pushkin's famous remark, 'we are given youth in vain'. Rather well put I think.

The terrible anti-sexual education that I received was really successful in that way, it just sort of blotted out possibilities. But I did have one relationship, only one, in college - with a fencing master actually. A young man who was connected with the university. I met him in London. But you see how very piano, how very reduced, this sexual life was. Everything was diverted into rugger.

I don't think that I ever really applied a label to myself, in the sense of being homosexual and not being anything else. I think I was bisexual. At university I had a relationship with a girl, in the town, which I think was a natural thing. I enjoyed it.

In the existing situation it didn't seem there was any possibility of marriage, never even crossed my mind really, because the class divisions were very severe at that time. They really were. I would have felt guilty in a sense, but you see, with women, it is something that you're allowed to do. This is the accepted male chauvinist pig business. The famous phrase of 'sowing wild oats'. A young man is permitted to sow his wild oats but what happens to the poor girl nobody knows or cares. That's why I did it, and didn't have all the homosexual relationships that I could have had. I think that was the awareness that my homosexuality was really sort of repressed. I can't even say that I was aware that I wanted it. No, I was not.

From Oxford I joined the colonial service and was posted to Nigeria. I was an Assistant District Officer, it's a standard thing that you are, which means that you can have all sorts of jobs; you can work in an office or you can work in the police or you can work as an assistant magistrate in the law courts. When I got to Africa I found that it was the normal thing, the done thing so to speak, to have a female, African prostitute. It was not exactly expected, but everybody did it. Unfortunately I got gonorrhoea, which was quite serious at that time because the cure was not so easy. And because of the gonorrhoea I thought, right, no more of these prostitutes.

I had a black policeman who was my personal bodyguard, because I was connected with the police. In fact, I had the status of Assistant Magistrate. Consequently I arrested people. I went down the road with a lorry full of policemen and arrested some chap, you see. And so in that situation I had my own personal policeman who was my bodyguard.

I went out into the bush one day with him. I planned this deliberately really, though I didn't admit it to myself at the time. And we slept the night in a little hut in the village, and then, of course, I had sex with him. He accepted the relationship quite naturally.

The relationship with this chap was, in a sense, a close relationship. I didn't think of it as such at the time; I didn't say to myself, I'm in love with this person. It hardly got off the ground. But, strange to say, fifty years later I think of that chap. I regret having left him as I was forced to do, and wonder where he is now, whether he's alive or dead or goodness knows what. The funny thing is that a relationship, which did not appear to me to be important at the time, comes up later in your life, fifty years later and you can't forget it.

It happened that in the town there was some kind of fracas, and a youth, about sixteen, stabbed somebody and killed him. This young chap was arrested, tried and condemned to death. I was flabbergasted. This particularly beautiful boy was hardly more than a boy, he looked like a lovely animal. And he was only sixteen years' old. But he had killed somebody and, as the law stood, he was guilty. The judge went through the whole process of the black cap and everything and solemnly condemned him to death and he was led away to be hanged. I was absolutely stupefied, I couldn't believe it. I went into the little office and there was the judge taking off his robes, and he said to me casually, sort of, oh David, would you like to play bridge with me tonight? And I thought, Christ. I was almost sick. And I think it was at that moment that I was condemned in my opinion that I really couldn't stay in the service. I often wonder now whether I should have stayed. I could have had a career if I had wanted, but I liked the blacks so much and I disliked the whites so much that I would have come unstuck, I'm sure, some way or other, if I had stayed in the service.

After Nigeria I really began to go adrift. I began to collapse. I took up a teaching job in a prep school and didn't like it. I thought, oh God, what shall I do? And very nearly went into the church as a monk. I was only about twenty-four. I used to have terrible waves of guilt. After masturbation I used to have cold baths and everything. God, I even went to Lourdes, I crawled up and down penitential steps and everything. Unbelievable. And at last, when I was really an old man, suddenly I threw it off. I sort of became independent.

I'm sure it had something to do with sex guilt. Absolutely. And a complete inability to get round this problem. How can you solve it? And you can't, you've either got to reject the church and arrive at the conclusion that there is nothing wrong with sexual life, or, if you retain the idea that there is something wrong with sexual life, then have no sexual life. All of this shows the terrible grinding conditioning, which you get during your education period, stays with you for life, until you finally throw it off. In fact, I don't think you ever throw it off completely. You can throw it off with your intellect but it remains, it hangs about, so to speak.

I never found a career. I didn't like teaching because of the discipline problem. So I left that and then I went into language teaching with the Berlitz school in Germany. Unfortunately not in Berlin where I would have met Christopher Isherwood, but in another place. I made contact with the gay movement for the first time in my life. At that time gay behaviour was more tolerated in Germany than it was elsewhere. They had a little Society for Human Rights, which was in fact the homosexual organisation. We used to have dances. For the first time in my life I actually danced with a man. That was 1929–30 and I was twenty-six.

This was just at the time when the Hitler business was beginning to appear in Germany. Incredibly, I had a relationship, not a sexual relationship, with a Nazi stormtrooper. He was in trouble and asked me if I could help him, because he had been caught by the police with a revolver in his hand and consequently he had been fined and he had no money. He asked if I would help to pay the fine, so I did. I met him once or twice and had cups of coffee. No sex. But strange to say, incredibly, his wife accused me of being homosexual and trying to drag him away from her, yes, and she reported me to the police. The police invited me to go to the station and be interrogated. They were very, very nice and they made an appointment early in the morning so that my employers wouldn't know. I went there and the policeman sort of asked a few questions, and he soon realised there was no problem and let me go.

Strange to say, at about that time these Nazi stormtroopers had a rally and stormtroopers came from the surrounding area to hold it, at the airport. The Graf Zeppelin was there and I went up to see what was going on. Nobody went except me. I was the only civilian among all these Nazi stormtoopers in their uniforms. I didn't know the first thing about it! There was a big white Mercedes going up and down reviewing the troops. Later on I realised that it must have been Hitler in his early days. I didn't even know who he was!

I came back to England from Germany because the job folded; the economic depression reduced everything. And then I took a most extraordinary step, which I've never quite been able to explain to myself. I went into the Guards as a guardsman. I often wondered why. There probably was a great mixture of motives. Among other things, I wanted desperately to make contact with some kind of society, social order. There is in the individual a terrific feeling that you want to belong to the society in which you live.

Strange to say, although I did have sex relations with three separate guardsmen, the chap that I really liked, you could say loved in a way because I had quite an emotional feeling, wouldn't have sex with me. He was a heterosexual type. He reciprocated on the level of comradeship. This is very important. Comradeship is permitted, and in the regiment there were pairs. I mean it was understood by everybody that so and so was the personal friend of so and so. Comradeship is allowed, on the understanding, of course, that there is no sexual relationship. No sex.

You could have sex with a fellow guardsman just like that, very easily, given the appropriate circumstances. You've got to be alone in the barrack room. You've got to be gay yourself and the other chap's got to be gay. Given that situation it happens just like that. These were not extensive or deep or even very close relationships really. With one man I think we had sex twice. On another occasion perhaps three times. In the third case there was something like a relationship. I mean we used to go out to the cinema together, so that there was a relationship apart from just sex.

You learnt very quickly to cover up any activity. This applies everywhere, surely also in civilian life; you can have sex with somebody, and then somebody else comes into the room, and with enormous expertise you immediately behave as if nothing has happened. And nobody thinks that anything has happened.

I think the reputation for male prostitution in the Guards has been blown up and exaggerated a bit, I mean it just wasn't true that all guardsmen were male prostitutes, I mean it was just not true at all. Some were, but I would say perhaps the sort of percentage that you would find in civilian society anyway. It was then that I did become political, because by chance Mosley was in the picture. And when I came out of the Guards I joined the Communist Party. I was in a little communist cell. Very upper class, actually.

I took part in the hunger marches also, but that is a different business. Yes, I actually went to Mansfield and we marched to Nottingham. That was a two-day march, we must have slept in a village hall on the way. I can't think why I did that, but I had one or two other little political experiences at that time. The Communist Party used to support strikes and if there was a strike on in London, I would go and support it.

I'm still a member. It was a thing that everybody did at that time. Nobody can believe it now. In 1935 it was quite the correct thing to do, be a member of the Communist Party. All the left-wing chaps in Hampstead were sort of communists. It was considered correct, because of the anti-fascist situation. It was now approximately 1936, I think, and I went over to Jersey. Where my parents now lived.

I worked at first in the potato fields. I even for a short time tried to grow potatoes myself. I married and I had a daughter. I taught in a school. And then suddenly along came the war.

Equally suddenly, after a few months, the German break-through, the French collapse, and, before you could say 'jack knife', the Germans were just across the water. My father said, crumbs, I can't stand this, and he took my mother by the last boat to England. My wife said to me, oh David, I don't want to go because the baby has just been born. She thought that it would be difficult or impossible to live in England, there were problems, etc. So, while we were dithering, of course the Germans just arrived and I spent the whole of the war years in Jersey.

In 1939 I had actually gone to the recruiting office and volun-teered. I said, I want to join the army. The man said, how old are you? So I said, I'm thirty-five, and he said, if you're wanted you will be called for, but you're really too old for the army as it stands at the moment. So I was a bit taken aback, I could hardly believe it. Me, old? I'm thirty-five!

By that time I was leading a double life actually, as so many gay men do. You get married and then you realise that you're not heterosexual really. Not only that, but also by that time, a differ-ent aspect of my life had begun to appear, the paedophile. It was from that point onwards that I began to get into serious trouble.

I'm sorry to say that I was incredibly stupid and during one such relationship I wrote a letter to the boy, which his father opened and look to the police. As a result, after I had been teaching in that school for twelve years, the headmaster said to me, I'm terribly sorry, David, but I've got to ask for your resig-nation.

My wife found out gradually. I think that she didn't immedi-ately realise at the start what sort of relationships I had had. And gradually it came across. There was a virtual separation between us from that point. She stayed in Jersey, I lived on the mainland. I used to go back to Jersey for holidays, etc., and so things continued for several years. Then, strange to say, her life came to an end, if you put it like that, in a rather peculiar way. She's not dead, but she lost her reason. I think the official name is premature senility.

I have a daughter and a grandson. My daughter is a very sensi-ble modern type of person and she doesn't have hang-ups about it. I have never told her about myself. She found out and gradually realised. Fortunately her life was not affected; her education was not spoilt as a result of my life.

I think relationships with younger boys are a different sort of relationship. Because of the age gap I think it is protective and, in a sense, parental. I think that it works both ways. It is a relationship, parental downwards and filial upwards. Just allow me to try to give you a little example of what I'm trying to say. In the middle of my youth, when I was only twelve, and under this terrific impression remember, at school, I was taken by my parents for a summer holiday. They had just come back from China. With us, in the same little group, was an old friend of my mother's who was a priest, a chaplain in the Anzacs, the Australian forces. He was on leave from the trenches in France. I liked him and he liked me, and he said to me come round and see me in the morning, any time. We were in this little village in Devon. And I got up at six o'clock in the morning and ran through the streets in my pyjamas and went to his place, knocked on the door, and jumped into bed with him.

We had a little, very fragmented, sort of sexual relationship and, you see, the question is, what sort of relationship was it? He was a man whom I admired, I was a boy whom he liked. We liked each other. And all this talk about sex seems to be a little bit off the point, because you see I wasn't really consenting to a sexual act. All this talk today about consent, consent, consent, can children give meaningful consent to a sexual act that they don't understand? I don't think that I was consenting to a sexual act. I was consenting to a relationship of friendship, call it love, if you like, in a rather general sense of the word. I was consenting to this friendly relationship, which I wanted and which he wanted. And the sexual bit was a sort of extra, in a sense. So what kind of relationship is it? It is a parental-filial relationship and, if you don't mind me sort of theorising about it, it's sort of para-incestuous. I don't think that anybody's ever going to come to grips with this until incest is brought into the picture. I don't think that society will ever successfully understand paedophilia except by understanding incest as well. Because that relationship was so much like a relationship between a father and a son.

The other day I was going down a tube on the escalator at Piccadilly, and a boy was going up the other way. He was on the game, and was heading for Piccadilly Circus tube. He was impressive and I couldn't help looking at him. I was going down the escalator and he was going up. I sort of looked at him and was admiring his beauty, and when he got to the top and I was at the bottom, he turned round, he said, do you want me?

In this situation, if I had wanted to, although I'm not terribly keen, actually, on that sort of pure pick-up relationship, but if I had said to him, okay, he would have come down and something could have happened. In that situation it would have been just a sort of pick-up relationship. There are paedophiles who do this, I know. Why shouldn't they? I mean, that's the way they feel and the boys want it, so okay, you know. I don't take high moral lines about prostitution. It seems to me to be a highly dubious area and I think that moral judgements are out of place.

I have not felt guilty about my paedophilia, actually. I know it is natural to me and I know it is natural for the boy. In fact, not only that but you could even put it round the other way. To tell you a rather peculiar little story. When I was working at a school in North London, from which I was eventually dismissed, there was a very attractive boy and I liked him, and he liked me too. I had a motorbike then and I went round to his house. He sort of begged me to take him somewhere for the Easter holiday on the back of my bike. His elder brother spoke to me and said, you know, Charles is very easily led, etc., etc. In fact, the brother was really asking me not to have any relationship with the boy, and feeling sort of something in connection with what is morally right and what is morally wrong. I thought to myself, oh well, the elder brother really doesn't want me to have a relationship with Charles, I won't, and so I didn't. And do you know, after that I felt guilty for not having a relationship. Because he wanted it and it was ungenerous of me to refuse that.

Oh I think that certainly I have felt isolated by my paedophilia. In a peer-group situation, if I am gay, then I mix with other men of the same age and, of course, this is a kind of social situation that can't be reproduced in the paedophile world. I think that there are all sorts of problems here. The whole area of paedophilia is very, very much more severely oppressed than gay relationships are. I feel that up to now nobody really knows much about the situation. Up to now the whole thing has been, and still is, so taboo. Necessary discussion has not even taken place. When human beings are trying to understand something, there must be an area of free play, in which the whole thing comes out into the open, so that a dialectic can take place in the conversation and points of view discussed. But if the whole thing is taboo nobody knows anything about it. And even the psychologists who are trying to venture into this area, can't get any response. I mean a psychologist who brings out a questionnaire can't even get anybody to answer his questions. The whole thing is incredibly taboo, and I don't think it'll ever be understood until it is taken in conjunction with incest. Why is there this hysteria? Why this extraordinary element of hysteria? Why is it that the parents go completely crackpot? Because they have repressed their own incestuous sexual feelings towards their own children.

6 A priest's life

Thomas was born into a professional family in Northumberland in 1907, and was educated at a public school and Durham University. He eventually entered the priesthood, serving abroad for many years, largely in Malaysia. After retiring, he tentatively began exploring his long-suppressed sexual needs. At the time of the interview he was living in the north of England with his unmarried sister, who knew nothing of his homosexuality. He continued to serve the local church.

I was born in 1907, in Northumberland. I was born prematurely, I believe. My father was a lawyer, so I was brought up in a middle-class professional family. I had three brothers younger than me, and then a sister and brother much later on when I was a teenager. All my surroundings were ordinary middle class. I went to a public school, and I had all the usual ideas of my class and time. Of course, homosexuality was something that wasn't mentioned at all really. Certainly I was talked to about it before I went to school. It was a time when Alec Waugh had just written *The Loom of Youth*, so that I remember my father was anxious, and I was told that boys did naughty things to each other and I must always be very careful, and not to associate with naughty boys .... Once, when Oscar Wilde was mentioned at the table, he was damned.

I don't think I really understood. I remember when I was having a bath as a child being told not to touch myself down there. And, in fact, the first time I masturbated was when I was about fifteen at school. I was terribly frightened about it. Then

I fell in love with another boy, and my great aim was to preserve him from any defilement. So it was all very romantic.

One started to masturbate and it was all secret and one was frightened about it. And then on holiday I went into a station lavatory and found a hole in the wall and all sorts of pictures on the wall. I was aroused, and started slipping away and visiting lavatories and looking through the hole in the wall. I was about sixteen, seventeen I suppose. I first met someone in a pissoir, and allowed myself to be tossed off. I felt very guilty. And I didn't like the man very much. But of course I had to go back.

One had been brought up to be manly and to despise any effeminacy. It was part of one's training, right from the wretched preparatory school where I went during the First World War and spent the most miserable time, because I was never good at games. Unless you were good at games you were not well regarded. I remember, as a very miserable little boy of about eleven or twelve, starting a fantasy about a rough man, before I even knew anything. I think it was through a book called *The Prince and the Pauper*. I began imagining myself being closeted with a rough sort of man in every sort of way, peeing on each other and that sort of thing.

One didn't know anything much about sex really. It was all hinted at. Once my father gave me a little book and said, you read this, and left me in the study to read it, and I couldn't make head nor tail of it, but it all made me feel that this is all rather awful!

It was not until I was at my public school, when we were dissecting frogs, that I really realised exactly how the sexual thing happened and I suddenly started blushing, funny isn't it? I'd already masturbated. One heard boys talking about it. And then, one night, I suddenly found myself with an erection and began playing with myself. And then I had this nice experience. But then I thought it awful and I tried to hide the handkerchief.

Fortunately, in my public school games wasn't everything. There was gossip in the school. We had what we called the college tweekies, and they were the nice-looking boys, little boys, who the elder boys rather used to like. It really didn't mean very much but it was a source of gossip. I don't know that they necessarily did it, but perhaps the older boys would go out with them surreptitiously. I don't know really.

When I left school I wanted to be an artist, and my father sent me to France to learn that I wasn't an artist. He was very sensible about me, poor man. And there, I went off with a young Frenchman once and we went out into the country. We had a rather unsatisfactory sort of affair, and then at home I gradually developed this second life.

I lived at home and we were very much protected, in those days, over-protected really. If my sister went to a dance one of us had to go with her, that kind of thing. In the meantime I was slipping off, having very unsatisfactory sort of affairs, perhaps just going down a side street into an alley and putting my penis between someone's legs or vice versa.

Well, of course, you didn't see yourself as homosexual, although I suppose I realised. I hoped that I was going through these phases. But anyway I got desperate. Then, suddenly, I actually had something that was more satisfactory but which frightened me more than anything. By going into a station lavatory and passing slips of papers under the wall, I got in touch with a young actor and went off to his lodgings in Newcastle, and there had the whole thing for the first time really. All the others had been very unsatisfactory, but this was lovely. We did everything.

At the time I felt, this is wonderful. But I was working in a lawyer's office, and read all the law about it and I realised that I was a criminal and could be sent to prison. And if my father and mother got to know it would be an absolute shame to them. I'd have to commit suicide or something. One heard of people 'doing the decent thing'.

I used to go into lavatories and look at people's cocks. I still find myself doing that actually. There were times when I got desperately frightened, you see. There was no way of really establishing a relationship with anyone because one couldn't speak to friends about it because you were frightened they'd be shocked. One desired, above all, to find a 'friend'. But one couldn't. There wasn't the possibility of it.

And so, one night I looked into a church and there was someone hearing confessions. So I went. The priest laughed. Afterwards he became a bishop; he was a remarkable man. And I started going to church and got carried away towards a vocation to the priesthood. Meanwhile certain things still went on, and I had to go back again and again to confession about this. I had nothing but help from the church. They were the most enlightened people at that time. They really were.

Then my poor father sent me to university. I took my degree at Durham. Things were easier there because I had many friends, and then I went to theological college. I had psychoanalysis actually. I used to lie on a bed and sort of associate - say what came into my mind. Sometimes I used to have awful urges to produce bursts of emotion. I think it helped, but what he did really was to try and lead me into heterosexuality. In fact, I did start going out with a girl cousin who I got very fond of. It didn't work of course. Fortunately. I had two years of analysis and then after I was ordained I still used to go, up until the war came and then the analyst was killed by a bomb, poor man, and it all faded out.

I've had a very happy ministry. And on the whole I've been able to remain celibate. But, of course, there were occasions when I wanted to escape, and, in various ways, I found some sort of help. Sometimes I used to go off into pubs to mix with men and there were one or two 'occasions'. It was all rather vague, you know. One thing that helped me in one parish was that my vicar joined the Masons and I joined the Buffaloes and I found a certain amount of help in the male society of the Buffaloes. At the same time, and all along, I've been cottaging, sometimes just to look about. It was a habit that would reassert itself from time to time. I think I saw it as a handicap. But it was something that, on the whole, I had been able to control and master, although it was always there, one was always on the edge of a precipice. One had read of bishops and people being caught in lavatories and one was just frightened and cautious. I think probably the Church stressed the danger more than the sin ... that is, of danger to the ministry. Did you know, very few parishioners came to ask advice about homosexuality? There were some who one knew were, and I think they nearly all went to the vicar.

The Church were the only people really who were sympathetic. There was a little book called *The Invert* by Anomaly, a Roman Catholic priest, and *The Difficult Commandment* by Father Martindale. There were quite a lot of religious works that were sympathetic. It all helped tremendously but I wasn't helped to realise there were many other people like one. There was no point of contact with anyone else. Celibate priests only owned up to it in the confessional. A tremendous help it would have been to have had a friend, another priest friend who was like oneself. Not necessarily to enter into any physical relationship, but to share one's experiences.

I think one hoped for someone of the same class, but in earlier days one was drawn to boys and men of the working class. I think there was a desire for toughness. I've always been put off by effeminacy.

One had heard that there were certain pubs where homosexuals resorted. I did live in London when I was in Camberwell and I certainly didn't visit any pubs. They weren't generally known about in 1931. Of course, I didn't go to Oxford or Cambridge Universities. Had I gone there I would have learnt far more about it, in those days. But I went to Durham, which was so much a provincial, and also very much a theological university at that time.

Then you see I went abroad to Malaya. I was abroad a long time and there the situation was quite different. In the Far East you don't come up against it in quite the same way for advice. There were occasions when one was asked to give advice about masturbation and, in that case, I had advanced from a rigid view to a more liberal view and the sort of thing I would advise was, well it's all right, but don't make too much of a habit of it, it may not be too good for you. I was in Malaya for twenty years. I ran a school in Malaya and I was always surrounded by young teenagers and one was able to sublimate for the most part. All through my ministry I've had a very happy time with so many people.

Of course, you never retire. I came home in '66 and retired in 1976. I've had a whale of a time since I came home. Though, at first, coming home in 1966 was frightful. My mother was dying and she'd gone a bit senile. I got to a parish, a mining parish in the north and, instead of being surrounded by children, I found children all crossing the road to avoid me. I got terribly depressed, I got into a frightful depression. I started going to public lavatories again. I went to my director, who again was an enlightened man. A Franciscan priest. In the meantime I'd read Norman Pittinger. I began to get a wider view. I was encouraged in that wider view by my spiritual advisers. I accepted it intellectually but not emotionally.

Then I went on a holiday to America. And there I broke loose. I went to New York, round to those porn shops, and then I went down to Washington for a couple of nights and there I met someone in a gay bar and took him home to a hotel. That didn't work. I hadn't been emotionally converted. The odd thing was that of all people that I chose it was a sort of hermaphrodite with a tiny little penis. Anyway, he was a nice chap.

Then I had awful repercussions. Guilt. And afterwards I kicked myself because I didn't even get his address to keep in touch with him, because he was a nice little man and he had taken pity on an old gentleman like me too, you see.

Then I imagined I'd got VD, because I'd been having a little old gentleman's complaint. That was in about 1972, I think. Then I read Tony Dyson's book *The Way of Love*. It isn't specifically about homosexuality, rather it is about love. And it was a very helpful book. And then there was an issue of *Christian*, on homosexuality. About two years ago I wrote to Tom Jones of the Open Church, and got in touch with him. He's a wonderful person. I think the Open Church is less politically activated than the Gay Christian Movement. It's not a large society really. There are only two of us in Newcastle—and one is not gay actually. But suddenly I was 'able' to accept myself. All the way along, there was this despising oneself and despising other homosexuals really at the same time, and to be able to come out and respect oneself and to respect and love other homosexuals was a wonderful experience. I've had no physical experiences but I am old. It's been like a sort of religious conversion I think.

I flew to God, in fear and trembling, to help me out of the position I was in. But after all my ministry I still believe, not in a God who's interfering, but I believe that behind it all there is some sort of plan. What it is, He only knows, but, on the whole, I think I would come down on the side that there is a meaning behind everything, rather than no meaning. I think this is so exciting and so interesting, do you see? Teilhard de Chardin and Freud himself have things to say about this. Freud said that he thought Eros would be the only thing that would save the human race. And Teilhard de Chardin talks about a new kind of love. I'm sure he was an orthodox Roman Catholic with regard to homosexuality, but he's not entirely orthodox because he believes that Eros can be used for something rather bigger than it has been used by man. I think that's true, isn't it? I've just been to a gay priests' conference, and I must say I was rather bored by it all. I feel we must be looking forward to how we're going to use this wonderful gift we've been given.

I think both heterosexuals and homosexuals today are rather too much concerned with just sex and not with relationships. The relationship is the important thing. What I feel, at least in my position, if sex will help, all very good. But my memories of casual sex are really not very pleasant. I feel if two people agree mutually to have sex, even if it's only for one night, then that's perfectly valid, if it's a matter of voluntary choice. I don't think that ought to lead necessarily to a long-term friendship or relationship. I just think there are so many different levels on which people can relate emotionally and sexually, and one doesn't exclude the other.

Being an old person I don't want to march about with banners. I think that there are two ways. Look at the suffragettes, there were the people like Pankhurst and so on who marched about, but they weren't the ones who really brought change. They had their place, and so have the gay processions no doubt, but really what is important is the individual. The leaven as it were. That's the thing in the end, because very often a lot of demonstrations produce the wrong kind of reaction.

I think my sister has an idea about homosexuality because she's seen books about it. I live with my sister and she's in fact my closest friend. My brother is ultra-conservative and talks about 'poufs'. I really don't want to cause family troubles by coming out to him. I came out with my bishop and he's very sympathetic and helpful ....

I don't think I would change my life. It had to be how it was and now no doubt it has been a wonderful thing, at the end of my life, to be able to come out.

7   An academic life

Trevor Thomas was born in 1907, in a South Wales mining village. From there he went to university and, at the age of twenty-two, began a career in museum work. During the war he became the director of a large museum and art gallery, where he inaugurated a lively programme of activities and events. He later married, had two sons, and went to work in Paris. Following this he went to North America where he made a reputation as an academic, writer and theatre designer. Back in Britain in the late 1950s he took his sons to live with him in London, and eventually moved to the provinces. In the early 1970s, after a period of loneliness and ill-health, he became involved with the Campaign for Homosexual Equality, and ran a helpline for gay disabled men. Retired, he now writes, paints and cares for his garden. The original interview was conducted in Bedford in 1978, and was supplemented by more recent conversations.

I was born in South Wales in a small mining village. My father was originally a miner, then became a winding-engine man. He was a kind, gentle sort of man. I had religious parents, Welsh Congregationalists. My father and mother founded and built their chapel, and I grew up going to the chapel three times every Sunday. Brought up very sheltered. Extremely sheltered.

I had an older brother, five years older. He was an athletic, sporting type. I was a rather good-looking, fair, blue-eyed boy with this extraordinary boy-soprano voice. So, of course, I was pushed round the eisteddfods singing, winning prizes all the time, from about the age of eight till my voice broke. I think that sort of thing has a curious effect on you because it sets you apart. You can become quite conceited and you think you are different, somehow. In fact, you are treated differently, you are regarded as a bit special, set to sit with the girls in music lessons because only you can hit top C.

And then, suddenly, at the age of about twelve to thirteen, my voice broke. I wasn't able to do this unique thing any more. That was a very traumatic experience. Because nobody explained why my voice broke or anything about sex. It was absolutely taboo at home. I was appallingly ignorant about it all. And here was my voice cracking for no known reason that I could tell. Except I related it to the fact that I was beginning to be aware of certain changes, you know, wet dreams. Again unexplained. I felt something must be wrong with me, that I was being punished in some way. I felt terribly guilty.

All this chapel thing was done in Welsh and I didn't speak Welsh. But I liked the singing, so I used to go along and engage in lovely daydreams. I was already artistic as a boy, with not much encouragement in the school. Again, I was regarded as different. The headmaster would hold up my drawings and say, these are marvellous, this boy is very gifted, etc. I wasn't allowed to go out and play very much with the other village boys.

Movies came in for the first time and they were shown in a tent, and you sat on planks. *The Broken Coin,* I think, was one and another was called *The Exploits of Elaine*, and *The Perils of Pauline*. We boys would act them out after, on our own. I was always either Elaine or Pauline, you see. And I had to be tied up and rescued by Eddie Palo. It was great fun, you know. But I didn't realise the significance of it, and there was no sexual contact going on. None of the sort of thing that most people remember having. I suppose there was some looking or something, but no physical contact. I had mainly friends of my own age, and mainly boys I think. There were some girls, in the street nearby in the village. But I didn't have a very wide acquaintance. I do remember having one boyfriend. I had a hell of a row with him, a fight, and then we became absolutely blood brothers, buddies. He took me home and said they'd got a medical encyclopedia. We looked at the diagrams and there was a little drawing of something. I'd be then about eleven I should think.

We had no bathroom so you had to have a bath in a tin tub in front of the kitchen fire. I assumed this was all very natural for a long time until once I saw my father having a bath in front of the fire, nude, and I was very intrigued. I never saw my mother, other than dressed, fully dressed. I assumed that it was inevitable and natural that a married man and woman had children and they slept together and this was the pattern without thinking about it really, I suppose.

I tended to be closer to my father, who was an absolutely charming man. Very fond of me. He'd take me round to the eisteddfods and he was very proud of the voice, and he sang a little himself. Taught me Welsh folksongs. My mother was the boss, the manager I think is the proper word, because she wasn't unduly aggressive about it, but she certainly had us all organised brilliantly. She was a professionally trained dressmaker. A very good one. And I'm sure I inherited a lot of artistic abilities from her. She made all my clothes right through to my late teens. The suits, everything, very skilful. She took great pride in seeing I was well dressed and looked smart. Apart from being strict she could sometimes be quite indulgent about clothes. They bought things that I think were unusual in a way, like oil paints for instance and canvasses. They knew there was something different in me. Though, I think, in a not over-aware way. One thing, my mother was determined that neither my brother nor I would go down the pits. Because that's the only career open, to become a preacher or a teacher or you went into business or down the mine. And I suppose I always think of myself as one that got away. Because I was a bright scholarship boy.

The artistic side of me always set me apart from my brother. But I never felt apart from my family as a whole. There was not a great deal of demonstration of affection between us. My mother would give you a rather dry hug. But she was always uptight about emotion, she didn't let emotion come out of control. I rarely saw them cry, or get upset. I seem to remember overhearing the odd row at night-time, but never openly in any way. I think my father was a very patient man. I was aware in later years that their relationship became more fraught. She could become cruel in her later years, often not realising she had been cruel.

I look back and I remember one particular very distressing experience. I was about ten, I'd just gone to the secondary school. My brother kept money for me, and I had to ask him for it. So I wanted some money one day at a lunch hour when we were allowed to go out and walk to the town. I went with another boy, while my brother was playing football, and we went to his clothes to get the coins. Then my brother found that a £1 note was missing and I was cross-examined by the headmaster, by my parents, by everybody, practically them all saying, you took it, come on, confess and it'll be easier for you. I kept saying, I didn't take it, I don't know anything about it. But nobody would believe it. Finally my mother, the only time I really saw her violent, lost her temper and she just hit me to the floor, punched, screamed, stomped and I was terrified. Absolutely terrified. And I never really trusted her, maybe no other woman, from there on. I'm sure that that was a turning point for me. I was ten or eleven.

There was another slightly traumatic thing that happened. When we travelled to school, the next station down there was a very jolly station master. We all loved him and he loved us and waved and chatted and so on. He used to say, come on Saturday and I'll show you the signals, and so a few boys would be invited to go and see him. He used to interfere with the boys. He had a nice little line. He'd take you over from the main station, across the line to the signal box. The idea was to show you how it worked, and you had to stand holding this lever which you had to pull very hard. Of course, you couldn't do it, and he'd say, I'll help you, and he'd stand behind you and he'd take off the brake, and suddenly you were released into his arms you see. And he'd have his hands around and all this, yes. And then his other line was to say there's a little mouse up your shorts. And then he'd take your trousers down and he'd like play and what he called kiss it. All this I found a bit alarming, but also rather exciting. He'd kiss you a lot with a rough unshaven face and I'd get my skin all red. When I'd got back my mother would say, what's the matter with your face? And I'd say, I don't know, it's hurting a bit, I think it's the sun. I never told them. But they had vague suspicions, I found years later. The other boys did tell their fathers, and he was dismissed, he had a lot of trouble. He had been interfering with Boy Scouts as well.

My fantasies at this time, as far as I can remember, were oriental fantasies. I was a slave and I had to obey the sultan or some marvellous wonderfully garbed oriental potentate. But I was a beautiful slave and I remember on wet days making my bed into a kind of an Arab tent, tying it to the four bedposts. I suppose you saw films and movies with fantasy situations. I tended to get cast always in these roles, even then in my mid-teens. Radio began to come in with the crystal set and I remember we had a debating society and we made a mock radio behind a sheet hung up with a microphone. We were behind it doing the voices. I can remember that as being a lot of fun, but not relating to it at all.

My brother first went to college. My parents paid for everything for him; he didn't win scholarships, they got no grants, and all from a very small income. I don't know what my father earned, about £6 a week, I think, in those days. My mother contrived to send my brother there, for four years. I was very aware of being thrown into her company a lot when my father was working, going shopping with her, see how she was managing. We were often literally without any money until my father's pay came in and so much was straight away sent off to my brother. All very brilliantly organised I think, I give great credit to her.

Then, when my brother finished, I was ready to follow him to Aberystwyth. My fees were paid. I romped home with the top scholarship in any of the Welsh colleges. My brother got a job as a teacher, lived at home and helped, so it was much easier for them and me.

I went to university with the intention of being a teacher, and this is where I, in effect, came out, or became very much more aware of my sexuality. I'd had vague feelings in my teens. When we'd been acting in plays, we'd be kept late after school. On the way back on the train the other boys would be necking madly with the girls. I would sort of withdraw into a corner and not want to, and get alarmed if some of the girls approached me. I remember having nervous twitches, if this girl comes near I don't know what I'll do.

On the other hand, I didn't have any boyfriend that I had any relations with. There were three of us who were friends, we were like the three musketeers, but we didn't play games. I've since found that both of these never got married and probably were homosexuals, and we none of us knew it or realised it, we just got along well together. At this time I wasn't even aware of my sexuality. I mean I had only vague ideas that babies were found somewhere.

I was aware that I'd go to these mixed college dances and I'd take these girls back after. We had to walk them home to the hostel, and it was the thing to kiss them and cuddle. Snogging on the doorstep. There'd be couples parked everywhere, and I'd sort of do a quick goodnight and beat it away fast. I'm sure the poor things were terribly disappointed I didn't find them attractive. I liked dancing, so I would dance. I suppose I would have really liked to have danced with the men.

I still didn't articulate this, at least not specifically. Other than in the context of a drag act in the smoker. There was a certain licence allowed in the smoker, as there is now in the East End pubs, a camaraderie. I would be in men's evening clothes, doing the man's part of it, and my friend would be in the dress.

About the age of eighteen to nineteen I did realise I was very attracted to men. But nothing happened. Which was sad in a way. I was becoming aware of the fact that in mixed gatherings suddenly there'd be a man I'd be talking to, perhaps, who would cause me to have curious physical stirrings, not necessarily getting a hard-on, just a slight dizzy feeling. Excitement. And also being a bit alarmed, what's happening, why am I like this? Later on, I found that in one or two instances I was having the same effect on them. I think this is what you don't realise or I didn't then, that you are, if you're homosexual, having an effect on other people who are finding you attractive.

I remember a man in the train, when I was travelling once, making some approaches and I really rebuffed him fiercely, you know. Not knowing why, just thinking that I was frightened about this man, that he would attack me in some way. He said to me, you dress very attractively, don't you? And I said, well I like nice clothes, my parents take care of it. He said, you file your nails. I file my nails, so what? He said, but you file them down to a point, that's very, very naughty! And I said, well I can't think what's naughty about keeping your nails trimmed, you know. I suppose vaguely I was beginning also to sense something sinister about him.

I'd got a degree by this time. I was supposed to get a first, but I suffered badly from hay fever. And I had it violent for the whole of one of the papers so I got a 2:1 instead, in human geography and anthropology. But my professor was very upset about this, and I think he therefore compensated for it. He took me on the staff as a junior assistant and then he later took me with him to Manchester as his assistant lecturer. But before that happened, once I'd got a degree, I had to have another subject to become a teacher. So I went off to summer school to do metalwork.

I arrived at this school and I was given a tent number to share with two chaps. To make a corny joke, I'd never camped before! It rained, and I woke up in the morning with a wet mattress, my feet were wet, and I was miserable. I went off to this office, to the secretary. I said, I'm not staying. And he said, well I'll come and see what's the matter. I said, well you look at it, there's a wet mattress and there's these two men and they snore and I don't like any of it. He said, oh don't be in a hurry, I'll see if we can find some lodgings for you in town. You go to the classes today and come back at four o'clock.

Well, I quite liked the metalwork part. I suddenly found this was something I liked doing. So I went back at four o'clock, he said, well you're very lucky, I've found somewhere and once I've cleared up the office, it'll be about five o'clock, you gather your things, and I'll take you along. Off we went to this house, met this nice lady who gave us tea, and then we decided to leave my things there and we'd go to the pictures. When we came back, she'd got some cocoa and sandwiches ready. At the end of the evening we went up the stairs to this bedroom, he opened the door, he said, well there you are. A real nice big bedroom with an old-fashioned brass bed, enormous, you know, typically Welsh, lace coverlet. And so I went in. I said, oh thank you very much. But he was in too and shut the door - it was his room! He was lodging there. And I was with him. And we got into bed and, of course, he started to make love to me. Assuming, looking the way I did, that I must know all about it. I was dreadfully upset. Because he fondled and kissed me and I thought it was awful. And I thought, God, now what's happened to me. I cried. Oh, poor chap. I cried my heart out, I was very distressed about it all, and he was very gentle, and he told me all about it. He said, you were longing for somebody to love you.

Of course I was lucky. He was about thirty, he was very sexually attractive and very sophisticated and we became very good friends. I did the course, I made all sorts of little ashtrays and what not, and learned a lot about metalworking. He took me home to his parents at the weekend to meet them. I took him home to mine who received him with open arms, what a nice kind man. His parents were well aware, he'd told them all about it. His mother was obviously very sympathetic, you know, and his father was a mining overseer and a very typical kindly man of the valleys. My friend was one of those chaps who hugged his mum, and they'd have long fond embraces and kisses. And I envied him in a way because if I'd tried to hug my mother she'd have said, oh, don't be silly.

The relationship developed into one of very good friendship, helpful friendship. That was in the summer vacation. Then, instead of going to be a teacher, my professor got in touch and said, if you like you could come back and be a sort of junior assistant. I did work in the library. I got the maps out for him, and did his diagrams and drawings. It was now that I went off to Manchester with my professor, and that was my first big city scene. My brother announced that he was now free to come back and do his PhD. He joined me and we shared lodgings together, to my distress, because in Manchester I soon found that, say, in the pictures or in the theatre, I was having approaches made to me and I couldn't do anything about it because of my brother.

One day my professor said, there's a job going that I think would suit you very well. It's in the museum in Liverpool, which will give you scope for your anthropology and your artistic abilities. I applied for this job and was interviewed and I got it. This was amazing at twenty-two to become a keeper of a department, and the papers went to town, the youngest keeper ever. Brilliant young Welshman. Very bad for your ego. And that's where I did work and did create quite a stir over the next six years, I suppose, creating a revolutionary change in museum display techniques. Up to that point in other ethnographical departments, the British Museum notoriously, everything was slung into glass shelves and the door was shut on it. I sorted it out and put it on cubes and made figures and used colours and so on. But I think the big thing there was that I was now on my own, really for the first time. I had a very reasonable income and was able to dress a bit more. I designed my own clothes and took drawings to the tailors.

I was becoming aware that there was a gay scene around, people you saw in the museum even, visitors, and you had to be a bit cautious. Careful. I still didn't realise that it was illegal.

I now found that there weren't many books either. There was a very limited range of knowledge available to you. The books that had the most influence on me were written by Edward Carpenter. Two things appealed to me, he was socialist, and he was writing about this thing, the idealism of male love, which comes across, I think, in his books. Then somebody told me about Walt Whitman too and I didn't go for that much, because I couldn't see the point there. I also read J. A. Symonds. I found this in a secondhand book shop, a thing called *In the Key of Blue*, and then *A Problem in Greek Ethics*. I got pretty shrewd at finding books but there was a very limited availability of information in the early thirties. I was very much a person who found out by books.

Not long after I'd been in my new job, one day I'd been stopped in the street by a good-looking man, whom I didn't know, who said, what a lovely day. And I agreed, it was a beautiful spring day. And he said, I like the look of you. Mutual, I like the look of you too. He said, would you like to come to my birthday party on Saturday? And I hesitated, then said, yes, I'd love to. And went, and it proved to be, to my surprise I must say, a party entirely of men in a private house. Roughly about fifteen men of all sorts, tall and short, and dark and fair, and some shy and some quite outgoing. And I realised this was what probably went on in small groups of people meeting ostensibly for birthday parties, very secret. It was all male. I was a good natural dancer, and there were such remarks as, oh this is the new one, have you tried him, he's really something. There was this tendency for people to say 'she' and 'her', then it was the 'it', where did you find 'it'? and so on. I disliked it very much, and still do.

In those days if you didn't find the key to the door to get on the inside you could be very lonely and very unhappy and not meet anybody. There were no gay groups, there were no clubs, there were few known bars. But once you'd been to one of those parties you got invited to others. And there were weekend parties at somebody's home, often when father and mother were away on holiday and the gay son would invite a few friends. But never more than eight, ten or twelve people. There'd be some dancing, some necking, some sex, going to bed, with more than one maybe. There was a tendency for these not to be outrageously obviously gay people: young businessmen, shop assistants, a solicitor, a teacher maybe, me, a museum man, tending to be rather quiet, shy people. No outrageous clothes. I think clothes were a very important distinction between then and now. You all wore dark suits, three-piece, very quiet shirts. To get a coloured shirt you'd have to have it specially made. I became known as the man who wore suede shoes. But I don't think they had that special kind of implication at that time. I found out about Liberty silk ties and I wore those, but my big alibis in all of this situation were (a) I was an artist, (b) I worked in the museum, and (c) I acted. And so these were your cover stories, alibis.

One of the opening gambits would be, are you fond of music? Do you like music? Oh yes, I like music very much. Oh, what are your favourite composers? And there would be double meanings as to whether, you know, if you were of the romantic slushy kind or the austere Bach type of thing.

I began to realise my homosexuality was a natural condition. On the other hand, I had to move around with a great deal of discretion, living the double life. The official museum person, with some very straight friends, and then the other secret life we led. I lived for a while with someone I met through my theatricals. If you'd looked at him initially, a schoolteacher, you wouldn't have thought there was any possibility of him being gay. We lived as a couple. I moved into lodgings with him, oh, for a year or so.

I had not had a lot of casual encounters. I knew nothing about the cottaging scene. I suppose I knew it went on, but considered it very risky. If I met anybody then it might start casually but then become a fairly steady sort of relationship. And then exclusive. I had another friend, I remember, in the theatre world. We couldn't meet very easily in the town, we went on holidays together, that kind of thing.

This first group that I went to, the birthday party, that group of people tended to meet quite frequently. They were once, when I wasn't there luckily for me, raided by the police and arrested and imprisoned. All of them. In some ways it made a funny story because a policeman crept up the stairs and listened through the door, and looked through the keyhole and then went in and arrested them, a mass arrest. In giving his evidence he said he'd heard somebody say, my, that's a whopper! And he's looked through the keyhole and he said when he saw what was going on he decided to go and arrest them. And they were charged in court. Of course, in those days, that'd be about the mid-thirties, a defence was out of the question. You couldn't say you were not guilty because you were on oaths you could swear black and blue but obviously you were going to be imprisoned, and many of those people I'd known, very charming people, very sensitive, were put into gaol, and really had a rough time. Their jobs, their careers, everything was gone.

That, I think, was the first time I began to realise that this could be a criminal offence, in some vague way. Though what was criminal about it I wasn't clear in literally legal terms.

I took a rented house, a small house, and let one or two of my colleagues from the museum have rooms. And then I met and fell in love with someone and he moved in and lived with me, and we had a housekeeper, and that was a very good relationship, for a few years. People were coming and going in the house, and getting married, but we remained as the sort of stable element. That brought me to 1938, that extraordinary year in my life, when I had now been recognised in the professional field and there was a big international congress of anthropologists to be held in Copenhagen, and I was made the Secretary of the section dealing with native arts. Then I got, one morning, this letter from America offering me a Rockefeller fellowship in a museum in Buffalo in the USA, and the chance to travel across country to see all kinds of museums, and to do surveys of the Pacific Exposition and the New York World Fair.

It was all a most amazing experience, arriving to the freedom of America. First of all I lived in a hotel and then gradually found an apartment. I was being taken up by the newspapers in a big way because I'd got my harp with me, and they wanted to know if I'd come to America to collect folk songs and I got photographed. As a result I got involved in concerts. Some lovely concerts. And in acting again with a little theatre there. I was the third angel in the Christmas play! I loved it all. I also found, through these channels, the American gay scene which was rather more open, even then. It was illegal, but the Americans seemed to be a good deal more open about it. Nobody screamed around the place, but you knew by instinctive feelings and looks. They loved you for the accent. I was always being asked to come to dinner, and bring my harp. The two pop songs of the day were 'Shuffle off to Buffalo' and 'I took my harp to a party, and nobody asked me to play'! They'd say, we'd love you to meet some of our friends. And the usual story, I began then to have more promiscuous relationships. Once you leave your own country and you're abroad there's the feeling that you're on the loose a little bit.

It was a year for this fellowship, from September '38 to September '39, by which time war was declared and I was in New York. I had still to finish writing my report on the surveys. So I went to the British Consulate in New York to know how I could go back home. And I was advised to stay where I was, I could, for the time being. They were advising all British nationals not to rush back. And the general mood was very pessimistic that this was the end, the lights were going out in Europe. Hitler will cross the Channel.

I came back to England in March 1940, in a convoy. I decided I'd volunteer for the forces. Somebody said you'd better go and volunteer then you can go into the regiment you'd like to go in. If you wait and they call you up they'll probably put you into the engineers or something. So I went and volunteered and that's a funny little story too. I went to this office, gave my name and address. And he said, well have you any particular preference for which service you want to go into? And I said, yes, I'd like to go into the Navy. Because I'd heard things about the Navy! And he said, have you any special reason? And I was joking, I said, very American, sure I think Navy blue and my blue eyes would look fine together. He was furious, he said, listen mister, there's a war on, no bloody nonsense.

Well, I went for a medical and they discovered I'd got defective hearing. And that was the end of that. I was told I would never be called up, I was the lowest medical grade, yet I was physically quite okay.

Then I applied for a job in Leicester as the director of the museum and art gallery. I wasn't too sure about getting that. In fact I didn't think I would, I was much too young. I was just, what, thirty-five. Very young for a directorship. So there I was, the director of this museum with the provision that I needn't do anything 'for the duration'. This was a phrase used a lot, everything was kind of in suspended animation.

Well, clearly I was very restless coming from America, absolutely bursting with ideas about display. All those American museums doing wonderful programmes for children. I stayed quiet for a little while. I then decided, having now got to know the committee, that we ought to move a little bit so I persuaded them that their collection of paintings and some other things were at risk. And they ought to be moved to a safe place in the country. Got that out of the way, that emptied some of the rooms.

I got in touch with the Arts Council, the Council for the Encouragement of Music and the Arts as it was known then, they had regional organisers, and we decided to try some lunchtime concerts at the museum, and changing exhibitions. The lunch-hour concerts caught on like wildfire, every lunch hour at one o'clock the place was full. Lovely artists came from London, for the day, early morning train, performed. I took great care of them. Got the WVS [Women's Voluntary Service] interested, they got a small food allowance and made sandwiches and soups. There was an outcry. Crumbs in the Art Gallery! But it worked you know, it went very well. I had a very good time. It was justified in terms of morale and holidays at home and saved people travelling, and to keep the children happy. The mood of the time was suddenly heroic. Once the raids started, everybody suddenly realised life was worth living, that we might lose it at any minute but it was worth having.

The other notable thing I did was to persuade the Art Committee to buy some outstanding examples of German Expressionist paintings. These formed the nucleus of what is near the best collection in this country. But the thing that I did that I remember with most satisfaction was organising the army art courses. Men waiting to be posted were often low in spirits and morale. I was asked by the Army Education Unit and the British Council to do trial runs with groups of about twenty men coming for three days. The courses went like a bomb. I realised I couldn't do much in a few days, but we could make it fun. When I was asked to do more I agreed, but only if they could come for a week. I insisted, and I won. They came for seven days. Even now, I sometimes hear from people who say the courses changed their lives.

Alas, something then happened that changed my life too, disastrously. Talk about pride going before a fall. I'd had a long, trying day in London, got back late, tired and frustrated. I went for a walk in a park, and in the gents I met the brother of a friend. We were simply talking, when two plainclothes policemen charged in, waving torches and shouting, 'gotcha, gotcha'. The police behaved badly, and we were kept incommunicado for hours, not allowed to contact a solicitor. I had made enemies among some of the more conventional and conservative officials like the town clerk and the chief constable. We were charged with a 'serious offence'. I still find it distressing to talk about it because not only did it wreck my career, but it was a situation that clearly illustrated the gross unfairness of the law then, even as compared with the still awful discrimination today. At least now it is possible to put up a defence.

The police behaved badly again after the preliminary hearing at the magistrate's courts. My friend left me alone while he went to find a taxi. Immediately, a policeman appeared and ordered me to follow him. The chief constable wanted to see me. I said, I'd have to wait until my friend returned. He said no, now, or do you want me to arrest you for resisting arrest? At the police station there was no chief constable. It was a ruse to get me on my own to take mug-shots and finger-prints, which was most irregular.

Afterwards, I was suspended from work, and had to surrender my keys. I became very distressed, and was looked after by various friends, marvellous people. The case was blown up into a *cause célèbre*. Important people came as character witnesses. The press had a field day. For me it was an appalling experience, as it did not go according to my lawyers' forecasts—a telling-off, a fine, a few months' 'special leave'. They had not allowed for a new judge on the circuit, and the town clerk. The maverick judge harangued me in particular and, as he grew red in the face, scattering sweat, spluttering and spitting, thumping his fist on the bench, he went on particularly about the need to save young boys from monsters like me. It began to look as if he were chastising himself, the need to save boys from him!

Then he threw the spanner into the works. He said he needed more time to decide what to do with us, so he was going to send us down for a weekend, to have a taste of what it would be like if, on Monday, he had decided to give us longer terms. This was a refinement of sadism for me.

I was in a near-hysterical state, and wanted to resign. The prison governor was a friend, and a member of our arts circle. He sent for me and said he couldn't understand what the judge was up to, but he would try to make my stay as least unpleasant as possible, which they did. Food was sent in, and I was allowed books and drawing materials. On Monday, the judge harangued again about protecting little boys, but he had decided not to send me to prison, because I would corrupt the others, which was indicative of his bias. He fined me £100, put me on probation on condition I saw the psychiatrist every week for a year in order 'to be cured'. Then, as I stepped down from the dock, the deputy town clerk handed me a buff envelope and insisted I opened it immediately. It contained a letter terminating my appointment immediately, stopping my salary and suspending my pension rights.

And there I was, in 1946, with the whole structure of my life in ruins. I honestly didn't know what to do. I hadn't a clue.

I sold everything I had practically. Some more or less strangers to me got in touch and said, we've got a holiday cottage in North Wales we're going to and we think you need a rest, would you like to come as our guest? I went for a few weeks, and then went to London and started up from there again. One valuable thing this horrible experience taught me was the wonderful goodness of loyal friends. It also taught me the decency of ordinary people, many of whom wrote to me. There were a few nasty letters, of course. What struck me significantly was that there were no messages from any religious personages, church or chapel, priest or preacher, none of them sent me any comfort.

I was now seeing the psychiatrist who had acted for me in the case. He was a Freudian, unfortunately for me. If he'd been Jungian he'd have probably said, go your way. Mine was quite an egoist and he 'knew' he could cure me. But we were getting nowhere. After six months of it he said, I can't go on any further, your imagery is too rich, and he tried to palm me off on to some Austrian woman. I had one session with her and that was enough.

I think he did believe he'd solved the problem, though, when I told him about this girl I'd met. I really believed I'd fallen in love with her, but had thought marriage was not for me. But he talked me into it. Of course, my parents now were delighted that I was going to get married and a lot of people in the profession said at last he's seen the light. I hadn't convinced myself I'd given up my homosexuality, I'd convinced myself that I could go the other way, and that then everybody would be so happy, you know, and it would solve a lot of professional problems.

I got a job with UNESCO, and my wife, my first son and I moved to Paris. Initially for a year. I stayed for eight years in the end. I kept strictly to the contract of the marriage, to begin with, trying to be a good husband and all that, and now the second child had come along. But I was beginning to have psychosomatic illnesses, near-breakdowns, tension. Back in England, after eight years, we lived for a while on the Isle of Wight, but it wasn't working. Then I left on my own for America, teaching in a college. When I said goodbye she said, go, go, I hope you never come back. While I was in America, she moved in with this man she'd got to know when she was in the Wrens. Somebody wrote nicely and told me about it. People always let you know. And that's when I made up my mind I'd stay in America.

During this time I didn't write to my wife. She wrote once when I cut the money. She said it was a cruel letter. I heard indirect news about the boys from my parents. They all wrote and said, you should come back. But I was having a wonderful time in America. I began to act, paint and design for the theatre again. We did a superb production of *Murder in the Cathedral*, in which I played the part of the Fourth Tempter. But in the end I had to come back, and try to make a go of it again with my wife. I had to think of the boys.

I got a job with a former colleague at UNESCO, publishing fine art cards. I was with them then, oh, fifteen years I suppose. Very happily, in London. I was living just around the corner from the boys' boarding school in a small apartment. I could see the boys every week and they could come at weekends and holidays. At this point I opted out of the gay scene. I'd been gay in America, quite actively so, and I'd come back and I'd got these boys, I decided, okay, I'm in London, I've got to devote myself to them.

I got some weird idea at the back of my mind that I ought to let them know about my homosexuality. But found that my wife had told them! They kept hiding from me the fact that they knew, and I kept hiding from them the fact that I didn't want them to know. It gradually came out one time and I just had to say, well all right now, I'll tell you the whole truth. You sit down and you listen.

My wife had now finally gone, ostensibly to be a housekeeper with the man she was with. After about two years she wanted a divorce. I agreed, as she was expecting a child. I got custody of the boys—and that was that.

Then my job moved to the Bedford headquarters as the London offices were to be demolished, and I decided in the end I'd have to come and stay. I found I wasn't very happy in what stuck me as a dull town. The boys were still in school, then moved away. I didn't see anyone even out on the streets who looked as though they might be even remotely interesting or fun to know. I was getting more and more frustrated because I was lonely. No sexual outlet, other than do it yourself. Visited by my boys, and, in due course, their wives and their children from time to time, and their crises. I was not painting much, not acting, doing nothing of that sort, reading, listening, watching television. Bit bored with the job. A limited existence.

I hadn't been aware of the happenings in the fifties and sixties, or the campaign to change the law, because I went to UNESCO in 1948, and I was there until 1956. Then I went to America and came back in 1961. Still trying not to be involved and quite unaware. I remember reading in the paper about something called the *Wolfenden Report* on homosexuality but was not very curious about it. And certainly unaware of the political agitation in 1967, the campaign to change the Act. It didn't seem to register much in my mind. I thought, oh well, it's legal now, you know. If this had happened years ago I wouldn't have been convicted. I'm not a political animal and, once the conviction had happened in Leicester, I think I was so bruised by it that I didn't want to know. Probably somewhere I think, deep down, I didn't want to know about sex even.

I had been feeling very unwell, I'd had the flu, I was very depressed and I was alone. I had nobody to look after me. I rang up the doctor, I said, do you think I could go to a rest centre for a week or so, just to have somebody to cook the meals and make the tea? I was there for several weeks. Meanwhile, my son told some friends of his in London about me and one said, well he must come and have a meal with us one evening when he's up visiting you. Well I went along, we got along very well, Elaine and I. I think she took to me a great deal, and said, next time you want to come to London you can always stay here if you want a bed.

While I was staying there one time, they're Unitarians, she was doing a stencil for the Unitarian magazine which she edited, and really slowly she said, Trevor, be an angel, go and get something for lunch. And I said, oh I think much more sensible, you go and get whatever it is for lunch and I'll do the stencil, I'll cut it for you, you know, in no time. Well, I started and I was going along and I came to the 'Campaign for Homosexual Equality'. And I stopped, you know, and thought, this is interesting. It went on about the oppression and the way gays were treated. When she came back from shopping I'd nearly finished, and, I said, well, fancy you asking me to do an article like that. It isn't a very good one, is it? She said, well why don't you go away and write a better one? I said, well how would I do that? She said, come on Trevor, we know about it. I said, well all right, I might do just that, and I did go away and write another article which they published.

I came back to Bedford and wrote off to Manchester for information. I got one of those leaflets, it was printed on purple paper but it was very good, I think those leaflets were better than the ones they do now. I found there was a local gay group. And I sent my money off to join, and they sent me a card saying you are a member. They took a bit of a while, and then one day this young man was at the door. I'm the secretary of the Bedford CHE group and we've had a letter from Manchester to say to get in touch with you, will you come along to a meeting? I liked him, he was from Canada. He came in and chatted away, and I said, well it's nice you're a Canadian, that's a bonus as well, and I've been in Canada, and we talked. I went to a meeting, and it was quite fun.

Then the next thing there was this conference to be held at Sheffield. I remember sitting there in the theatre, looking and thinking well, I'd estimate there's about seven, eight or nine hundred people here. And all here for this thing, so there must be something about it. Then next morning, of course, they had speakers and I thought, well this is a good thing, I won't rush home yet, I'll see a bit. And they were all lined up on the platform. It's all very new to you your first time, and it was very good. On the Saturday morning after these speeches there was a bit of business, and the chair said, well now, the next item is disabled gays. And I said, I want to speak on this, about disabled gays, waving my walking stick.

I got up and I said, I'm an elderly and a disabled gay and I've been here and I've been listening and there's some tension underneath the surface of all this. You're all hating each other instead of loving each other. I don't know why. But you can't brush disabled gays like me under the carpet, we've been around a long time. I got a bit of applause. And then people started to come and talk to me a bit. There was the disco in the evening; the cheese and wine I thought was my deal and I sat bold as hell at the cheese and wine, thinking, oh this is terrible. And there was a pretty poor drag show on, somebody pretending to be Marlene Dietrich. And then I wandered up some stairs and found myself in the disco and I went and sat. Ah, this is more like life, you know, but I don't dance, I'm disabled. And then two boys from Brixton, they came and sat next to me. I had long hair, and the Irish boy, Colm, kept doing this, fiddling, and he said, your hair's lovely and soft, and I said, well yes, you can leave it alone. And then the other one said, come on, throw your stick away and dance. I said, no, I'll fall over. He said, you won't, we'll hold you up. And they grabbed me. And I was on the floor. Well, I used to dance a lot and I thought, well I'd better do something and I liked it a lot. I came out then in effect. I danced around. It was fun.

Next day, this newspaper man said could he have a few words? I said, well what do you want to talk about, who are you? He said, I'm from the press. I said, oh no. I said, well who are you from, *News of the World* or the *Daily Mail*, or what? He said, no, the *Yorkshire Post*. Okay, that's a bit better, the *Guardian*, the *Post*, I don't mind. So he said, I just want to know how you feel. You're obviously the oldest person here, are you envious of these young people and their freedom and what was it like when you were young? I said, of course I'm envious of them, aren't you? Because he was pretending he wasn't gay and, of course, he was. And then he said, can I quote you? And I said, do you want to give my name and where I come from? Yes. Oh dear. So, I said, okay, yes, I don't mind. So what. And so the Monday morning the *Yorkshire Post* had it, you know, quoting Trevor Thomas from Bedford.

But the real crunch came that morning. At the main meeting there was a riot. A woman said that women were getting a raw deal, and she was lonely. Then the young people rebelled and walked out. And then this young boy stood up and said, I'm fourteen and I'm gay and I shouldn't be here.

I was waiting to speak for elderly gays. I was sitting in the front ready. He jumped down and I grabbed him. And I don't know what suddenly came over me, I've no idea what happened to this day. I'd prepared some notes and I threw them away. It was as if I'd been taken over literally by some force and said, now you stand, wait, because it's not true, we do love you, I love you, I think you're very brave at fourteen to stand up. I wouldn't dare do it. I'm the eldest here and you're the youngest and they're in-between, all the others. And they are hating each other and they shouldn't. You're here to love in your way not their way, and not hate.

And I kissed this boy. Of course, the roof went off. Everybody on their feet, stamping, shouting. The tension broke, you see, it was like it was on the water, and suddenly all the feelings were out. It was emotional, if you like, it was traumatic. It had done something. I was now 'out', and couldn't have been more obviously out, if ever. I've summed it up in the phrase that three days in Sheffield did more for me than three years on valium.

8 A Londoner's life

*Roy was born in Brixton, South London in 1908. His parents were poor,
but he had a strong family background, keeping in touch with (but keeping
his homosexuality away from) his parents, brothers and sisters all their
lives. During the inter-war years he worked as a dental mechanic, then in
the gas works in London. In the evenings he worked for a while in the
theatre, mixing with theatrical people. After a lively war, a large part of
which was spent in India, he returned to London, eventually buying a house
back in South London, and started letting out rooms. In the 1970s he
moved to Manchester, and became an active member of the Campaign for
Homosexual Equality group there. It was in Manchester that this interview took place.*

I was born in October in 1908, in Brixton in London. I remember Brixton very well. I think what I most remember is when the
theatre came, the Brixton Theatre, they would all parade down
the street, in their costumes to make the people interested.
Consequently my mother was very fond of the theatre, and I
got taken often. Some of the old actors or actresses, even Ellen
Terry, I've seen her act, and people of that age.

I come from a poor background. But that makes me think.
My father worked in the Gas Company in those days, and he
was an ordinary stoker. But I just don't know how we managed,
because since I've been in the North, I hear the most dreadful
stories of poverty. We were never in poverty. Even when I was
a teenager there was so much food in the house, believe me or
not. I hear terrible stories of friends in Manchester, Lancashire,

or even Yorkshire, in the days before the war when the depression was on, they tell me they had absolutely no food, they didn't know where the food was coming from. They lived from hand to mouth. We never did.

We always had a holiday at Ramsgate. There used to be a boat go from the Tower of London called the Royal Sovereign. It was a cheap trip. Not a very pleasant trip. And so we all went to Ramsgate for one week's holiday.

My mother never worked in her married life. Everybody goes to work now, wives go to work, and they still haven't got any money. But we used to go to the theatre. And when I think of it, as I got older, even as a schoolboy, the pubs were always full. So that's something which I can't explain.

Then my mother began to take theatre people in. The theatre. I think that's where I got it from really. My mother could tell you many stories of the funny things they used to do.

I know my first experience of being gay. I was very, very young and I went to the cinema. I think my parents must have been very easy with me because it was night time. I should have been at home in bed I expect, but they didn't mind. I don't know how it was but I went to the cinema and sat next to a soldier. He began pressing my leg and then he held my hand for me to press his leg like that, and I must admit it was rather pleasant I knew that I shouldn't be doing it. And then the next thing my hand was over his prick which had the horn. And I played with it. And then the next thing, it was out. And it almost seems, hard to believe this, but it always seems it was only two or three years ago, it was so vivid. I think I was about twelve. I suddenly got frightened so I must have had a guilt feeling. And I remember I turned away. He did nothing to me and he walked out of the cinema. I went home.

I think that if my parents had been up (they'd gone to bed) I would have told them. That's the most extraordinary thing, I think I would have told them. But my brother came in and I decided not to tell him. That was my first reaction.

I didn't go again, it was a thing that had happened and passed. The next thing was in Brixton. There was a wide open space, opposite the Prince of Wales pub, a very big pub in Brixton, which is still there. People used to come and sell things. They used to gather round because they had a little lamp, acetylene lamp which made a bit of light. It was not a very big light and I'm standing like this, I remember very well, looking and interested, and a man was pushing himself into me. I'd got my hands behind my back. I thought, this was lovely. I suppose it was then I realised that I was very much that way. I went many times, but if ever they spoke to me, I flew. I was frightened.

In those days sex was not mentioned. My mother used to make a joke, she never swore and never drank, but I remember she would sometimes say, like a silly joke, once upon a time, Fanny was a girl's name, and we thought that was very wicked.

At school—it was just a London County Council school—I sat next to a boy whose parents had a greengrocer's shop and he was always taking it out and wanking it and I used to look. As a matter of fact the teacher saw it once and said, come out here. He knew what I was doing. I was looking at Tut, I remember his name. 'Well, why were you looking at him, what was he doing?' 'Nothing.' 'Oh you were just looking at nothing?' You know, I was embarrassed, but anyway I wasn't going to say, I was looking at him wanking himself! Yes, I suppose I enjoyed all that.

I went out to work at fourteen. I was working as a dental mechanic's assistant. I didn't like it, but I used to have to take the tram to Victoria from Brixton, and then walk across Green Park, and up Bond Street, to save money. Then I started going to the local pictures and met people and went back to their house. I remember the first time I was stuffed, which hurt very much and I was a bit frightened the next day. I was about fifteen. That's when I began to realise that I was that way. I never thought whether it was right or wrong. All that bloody nonsense now where people think it's right or wrong, it was just something. Didn't occur to me about anything else.

One of my jobs in the dental mechanic's was to take the dentures out to the dentists. I was always up and down Harley Street, Wimpole Street and Welbeck Street. You rang the bell and the butler opened the door. They were larking about then, being a boy of fifteen you see of course, they would, 'come on, let's have a feel' and do that. Once I had to go up in a lift, and the butler was a bit of a nuisance. I do remember we used to go home at night and walk down Bond Street with the senior mechanics. I remember saying, oh that man, he keeps on touching me up. And they said, well he's a dirty old man, you shouldn't let him do it. And I thought, that's what you think! It was then I realised it was wrong. I used to go into cottages. I have always been in cottages. There was a very famous one in the middle of the road in Brixton, although I never thought of 'famous' cottages. There was plenty of them attached to the public houses in London. I don't know if they've still got them, they certainly don't have them here. But there used to be a stinking little cottage. This was a green metal cottage. There were always people in there, always. And there seemed to be a lot of soldiers about in those days. They had to wear their uniform, which they don't do anymore, unfortunately!

I took my aunt out one night to the theatre and we went to the gallery of the old Prince of Wales theatre. It's been tremendously altered now. We went to see *The Ghost Train*. We were in the gallery and I realised then, my instinct. Nobody told me. I kept on looking at the back and it was jet black, and crowded, crowded full of people standing, although there were a lot of empty seats. And that was, I think, my first realisation that this was a scene which I wanted to join in, I went back two or three days afterwards to see *The Ghost Train* and stood at the back and what was going on there was nobody's business!

They were big meeting places. You did meet nice people in those days, something you don't do these days, and wealthy people too. They were not nasty people. They'd probably give you a whisky, which I thought was nice. Never occurred to me to take money. Just never occurred to them, I shouldn't think. It never occurred to anyone. I went round these theatres quite a lot.

Then I went to the London Coliseum and I'm now about nineteen, getting on for twenty in 1927–28. I went to the London Coliseum, and met a man whose name was George and he worked at the Claridge Hotel. He lived in Kilburn, and I lived in Brixton. Imagine the distance, you couldn't even afford to go now, with the price of the fares! He said, would I go back with him. And I did because the buses were running. I always went home after, always, I never stayed out. I don't even stay out now. I don't like staying out. In the summer as soon as the dawn comes, I'm home, like Cinderella. I liked him very much. He was a man of about forty-five, forty-eight. I thought he was a much older man. I went again to see him, and a great friendship sprung up, very quickly. I'm only talking about two or three visits, and he said I would like you to meet my friends, and they would like to meet you. So we arranged to go over there. They all said, well we'll have a party. That was in the old days, a party mind you, a marvellous party. And then that struck me. Well, we've got to do something for this room. And they all sent out and brought paint brushes and paint, and painted the room red and green and everything. I lived in a world where you had either distemper on the wall or an ordinary proper pattern, but this was all madness. That was the first time I'd danced with another man and that was when I arrived into the gay world. That's when I knew exactly what I was. Because I enjoyed it so much, I enjoyed the dancing and I enjoyed the company. I remember they used to say, oh I had a lovely time last night, I got stuffed. Fancy talking like that? It's terrible. I was greatly excited, it was a marvellous world. Especially with the friendship.

I was travelling all over London. I think if you had fourpence you went all over London in those days. We used to meet in the pubs. They all liked port wine funnily enough! We used to go to the Dickens in Edgware Road, and 'JB's', Jack Bloomfield's, right opposite what was then Daly's theatre, which is now Warner's cinema. Some pubs were raided sometimes. They would just come in and take all your names. And that was the end of the pub, nobody went there again.

We were 'so'. Have you ever heard that word? We were so. Is he so? Oh yes. Oh he's so so, and TBH (to be had) was a very famous expression. The sentence would go simply like this, well he's not really 'so' but he's TBH. And you would know exactly. I don't know when I first heard the word homosexual. I always remember somebody saying, oh she's a lesbian and I didn't know what that meant. I didn't think women did that thing!

We used to go to Shepherd Market. And there was a pub called the Running Horse. It was years ago, I was very young. Perhaps twenty-one. It seems such a long time ago, most things seem quite new to me but this seemed such a long time ago. And at the bar was a lesbian. I didn't even realise she was a lesbian, but Ernie, he said, oh she's a lesbian. Her name was Radclyffe Hall. She wrote *The Well of Loneliness*. She fascinated me. Being young, she must have been young too, she liked me and I liked her. She wore men's clothes, and that's the only time I've ever seen it. Perhaps sometimes a skirt, but I've even seen her in men's trousers, I thought it was terrible. If she wore a skirt it would be black with braid down it. But always a man's evening coat, and a black hat and a monocle and this long, long cigarette holder. Talk about sophistication, it wasn't true! She must have been writing *The Well of Loneliness* at the time because I remember people used to pass it from one to another and I thought it was a beautiful book. Why they banned it I do not know, but of course it's allowed now. There wasn't many books about homosexuality to read then. Havelock Ellis, I read, but as far as I know they were the only books which was any good. Everybody had to buy it and everybody had to get it.

I think you're born to it. Completely, without any question at all, you cannot beat it, you cannot have any psychological treatment, you can't have anything if you're that way. You are that way, and my life I would say, could not be altered. And by the way, I have had women when I was in the theatre.

I was a bit of a snob probably. They had to be tall, they had to be elegant, and they had to have a good voice. You know I used to like them but if you knew them for a long time they would want you to go to bed and have sex, and I could never seem to get the bloody thing in anyway! It was always a bit of a failure. I have, of course, got a strong hard-on. But I didn't know what the bloody thing was, it was all foreign to me!

People used to help each other. It's very important, they don't seem to do it these days. I remember once I met someone and went back with him. I was suffering from sinus problems, and he made arrangements right there and then to go into the hospital. It was through him I had an operation.

I'm trying to say how interested people were. You know, in those days they all helped you. This man, George, he heard of this job. And they said, there is a good job going as an assistant in the box office. I said, well I'm working, I've got a good job. And they said, oh well, work in the evenings. And I got a job there, and it was from there I went into the theatre side.

And so I went there, and my job was then as a kind of receptionist. I was dressed up in full evening dress. The tails and white gloves and everything. I stood in the middle on a dais and directed the people to their boxes, and to see they had their hat on, or hat off, and I had to be diplomatic. I also had to be diplomatic to meet the critics, and put them in their seats. Women could not wear a hat of any description in the stalls. So if a Duchess had got two seats and she didn't know what to do with them because she couldn't go, she'd give them to the cook. The cook would come and I had to have the diplomatic job of directing them into the upper circle, because they wore a hat or something like that. And vice versa. Sometimes people would have a ticket and they were too well dressed to go in the dress circle or in the upper circle, so I would have to say, oh I'm sorry madam, I'm sorry sir, but there's been a duplication with your tickets, and take them to either the best seat or not such a good seat. That was my job. You had to be nice, but I say, even to this day, the critics, the bastards, they used to sit in there and get drunk, and then give a rotten report on the play which they had never seen.

I was there quite a long time, and still worked at the gas company as well. I got very friendly with the manageress, who was evidently a very great friend of the theatre owner. She was having it off with him, and she liked me, and I was having it off with her! She was very nice.

The theatre was very gay. I was almost always off my duty post, I was always round backstage. They had a bar then, as a matter of fact the manageress got so fed up with the bar eventually she did away with it.

If you went to clubs in those days before the war, you'd have been arrested and put in prison. I know personally a case where a woman, who I knew very well, started this gay club. Now I am talking many years ago, before the war, and I could see the danger. I said, you've got to stop it. But she took a house in Holland Park. It was known as the Holland Park case. They just danced, nothing so blatant as they do now. And one Saturday night the whole of Holland Park, reaching up to Shepherd's Bush I should think, was simply full of black marias and police. People thought the war had started or something. And there were two young policemen who were dressed up. Of course they gave the evidence. And everyone was arrested.

Now what I'm saying is history. They took them all to Brixton prison. And kept them there, they were not given bail. When they went up to the Old Bailey, it was top news, they had placards then, you know. The *Evening News* used to have a placard on, and everyone was talking about it. The judge made them wear a placard. He said there's too many to deal with these terrible people, put a placard on them and a number. And so they were numbered, with the indignity of this bloody placard. And then the trial came to the time of the sentences and he sentenced them to imprisonment.

When it was all over, the judge called these two detectives and praised them. He said, I am going to recommend your promotion for dealing with this horrible case. I feel so sorry, it must have affected you mentally. And I direct now that under no circumstances must you ever be involved in a case again of any description with homosexual men because no human being could stand it. It just shows you the scathing bitterness they had for it.

I stayed in Brixton until the war. And then, of course, it was bombed, blown up. Oh yes. I was away and my mother and father went to Oxford to live and my sister and brother stayed, but when the bombing came they left and went back to Oxford. I was in the Royal Army Medical Corps. Oh now we're on to the war, of course as somebody said to me, she said, I hate to say this, Roy, but I must tell you, she said, it was such a lovely war. Oh what went on was no one's business. And I went to Edinburgh, I was stationed there—I got on very well. Very well in the army, I loved it you know. Went to Edinburgh, the place was a riot, a riot. And, even London. I was on leave, I was pass-

ing through London. Bloody bombs come falling all over the
place and there was a Canadian, a little Canadian, and he said,
where do I go? And I took him to the Salvation Army and they
shut the door in his face because he was drunk. I said, what do
you mean, the bombs are falling, the shells, the shrapnel. Can't
help it. So I had a booking for the Union Jack Club across the
road, in Waterloo, and look him across there. I said, you follow
me. So he slept with me that night. He was willing, he was TBH.
I know a lot of married men, I used to have married men. Yes,
Edinburgh was a tremendous city, it was so full of sailors and
quite easy, quite, quite easy. The place was as if the world had
gone mad because it was so easy. But that was Edinburgh. Then
I was stationed in Sussex, in Goodwood as a matter of fact, in
Goodwood House. Somebody said to me, well, fancy you living
in Goodwood House, how lovely it must be, you are fortunate.
Well, I said, I'm very fortunate now because a little while ago my
bed was where the dog slept. But now I've had a raise and I've
got a lovely horse stable. Which I had. But it makes you laugh,
doesn't it?

After the war, I met a man in Edinburgh, called Bill, a character of a character. He was always so well dressed, always
immaculately dressed. He wasn't well off, but he wasn't poor.
We went back to London because he had his flat there, he was a
civil servant. A man very sure of himself, very kind, would do
anything for you. Anything. And a most overpowering man,
when he wanted something. We went around to a friend who
was very desperately ill once. He lived in this hovel of a place
and Bill said, put something on. And we got a taxi and took him
to the Hammersmith Hospital in the casualty. And they said, oh
well he had to go back. And I remember Bill saying, no way will
I take him back. And if you want to take him back you take him
back in an ambulance, but you won't get in, so what are you
going to do? No way. So the surgeon went and called the
Matron, he put it in her plate. She said, there's simply no room
for him to be admitted. He said, I don't care what you say
Matron, then he'll stay here. And they put him in a private ward.
But that was Bill.

I went to India, and had a good time there. Then, back in

London I met my first real affair, where we lived together and I was extremely happy, very, very happy. For two years I was living in this flat paying rent and my friend, he came to London and he said, well don't you think you ought to make a start and do something better? And a friend, Jimmy, who was a solicitor and gay as anything, it was him who pushed me - he simply pushed me. He got me this house in a slum, which turned out to be the happiest house I've ever been in, but my affair wouldn't go there. And it was the last moment, and this was a man who I was so fond of - it was unbelievable - but at the last moment he didn't come. He just left. Because it was a slum. It wasn't suitable for him. But now he regretted it afterwards. And that was my first venture into this business of letting rooms.

I never lived with a person again. But I used to have friends. But I always had a lot of trade, always. Oh no, no great problem. Now, of course when you get to my age now, it seems funny you can't realise you're old, do you know tha?. Except sexually. Then it becomes, you know. I saw my doctor about it. I'd had this operation for prostate gland, and I believe it, one of those things that three-quarters of the operations are enormously successful and makes your sex life even more powerful. Or it can go the other way, which mine did. And, but I enjoy sex of course, but not like in those old days when, ooh, you know.

The youngsters today could look for something better, but they don't seem to bother, do they? A funny crowd I always think, they've never got any money. In my days it would be unforgivable. Nobody said, I haven't got any money. If they hadn't got any money they wouldn't go out because it was a loss of status. I also was surprised when I first came here to Manchester that they used to say, what do you work at? Oh I've got a stall, I'm a window cleaner and all that. As far as I know, in London I never met anybody asking that.

I made an early retirement and moved up here to Manchester. I think it's a ghastly place, London, now. Manchester was quite gay, much gayer than London, then, immediately after the 1967 Act. Now I don't think so, but then it amazed me how open they were. Of course, it's the first time in my life I'd seen drag walking along the street. In London you would get arrested. But lots of them were doing it. I'm not talking about an odd one here and there. But that seems to have stopped now. If they were working class in London they would never admit to it, not in London. They do in Manchester. You know, they would easily here say, I'm out of work, well I think most of them are out of work here. As far as I can remember nobody was out of work when I was younger. Somebody used to say, a funny thing about gays, here we're in a depression, and yet if you buy a couple of drinks you always take a pound note out, and if you notice it's true.

My family never got to know about my gayness. Mind you, my sister died only last year and I often think if she didn't know, well what was wrong with her? But she never said anything and neither did I. No, they never knew. Do you know, even today I find, if you're talking to normal people, they don't like talking about gays. Have you ever noticed that? So imagine what it was like then. It was an unmentionable subject.

Joining CHE became one of the finest things I've ever done in my life. When I first went to a party and met these CHE people, that's where I first went into the scene properly and knew that this was my life. When I joined CHE I did feel, if I might say so, quite popular. For the five years before I was very much out of it because of my age. But with CHE and knowing people, I know plenty of young people and they're very pleasant and kind. I am treated very well.

9 A South African life

Cecil was born in 1909, of middle-class parents then based in South Africa. For half his life he lived in South Africa himself, and was a leading actor and producer there. He became heavily involved in left-wing politics during the 1940s (he joined the South African Communist Party) and then, after the Nationalist Party victory in 1948, in opposition to the new apartheid policies. Banned under the Suppression of Communism legislation, he continued working underground until arrested, with Nelson Mandela, in 1962. After a period of imprisonment he was put under house detention, but escaped and settled in Britain. In Britain, he resumed his drama teaching and producing career, first in Scotland, then as a freelance in various parts of the world. He settled with a younger lover, in a relationship that lasted some twenty years. The interview was conducted in Cecil's home in North London, shortly before his death.

I was born in Cornwall in 1909. In point of fact that was accidental. My mother was away on holiday and that's why I was born there, otherwise I'd have been born in South Africa. When my mother was pregnant with me she wasn't well and my father sent her back to Britain. So that's how I came to be born here, which many, many years later turned out to be a definite asset to me. Both my parents were British but independently had gone to South Africa, had met there and married. After a few months I went back to South Africa. Then when I was four years' old my parents came back to Britain, and so I spent the rest of my childhood, school-days, and even started university, in Britain.

Looking back one can pick up various traces of a homosexual personality that one is quite unaware of as a child. For instance, I can remember when I must have been, I don't know how old, nine or ten, going to a pantomime and being very, very struck, in a sentimental way, with the handsome hero of the piece. Then I had sexual experiences with somebody who was older than me. I think he was in the Boy Scouts or Wolf Cubs. I was a Wolf Cub then. I must have been eleven. The interesting thing is, of course, that it appeared to be a compulsion; the point is, of course, that I went willingly.

I didn't make a report or tell my mother about what was going on. It went on for some time. We were fairly close neighbours and we were living in a small town in England where you know practically everybody. I remember he lived just up the road from us. They had a kind of summer house in their back garden, so that was a rendezvous. I remember on one occasion he tried to persuade me to touch up one or two other fellows.

After the affair it was a considerable lapse of time before I became sexually aware myself. I became aware of masturbation. I can always remember my mother, my father was away then, in vague terms warning us of the terrible disasters that would occur if we did certain things. Really, I smile when I think of my mother, it must have cost her tremendous effort to approach such a subject herself. I was a Wolf Cub and there was that terrible tenth law, which says a Scout is clean in thought and word and deed, and there was only one deed in which I could think of myself as being dirty, and that was in masturbation. I understand that the Scout laws have been changed now. But I know for years I masturbated and tried not to. For there was the feeling of guilt and the fear of consequences.

When I went to college I met someone. We lay together and played together, which in recollection was very nice indeed. I remember asking him how did he come to know about this business of being in bed with somebody else, because it was a new experience for me. And he told me that he'd been at a boarding school, and obviously that's where he started doing it. I can't remember us discussing and comparing notes of our feelings or anything like that. I don't think that happened. It was just pleasant lying together really with the sort of sexual play. I was at that college for one year, because then I went to South Africa, and this probably didn't happen until the third term.

Then I went to Johannesburg. Walking away from the university one evening, I presume I had been to a rehearsal for the dramatic society, a man somewhat older than I was got into conversation with me, and from that he invited me to his flat. Really I am amused when I think now, because don't forget I had lived all my life in Cornwall, and in a small town at that, and here I am in Johannesburg and the mere mention of the word 'flat', 'my flat', the connotations were fabulous and inevitably you know all sorts of unspeakable things went on there! However, I went to his flat and sure enough it had shaded lights and lots of cushions on the divan, and there came a time when he undid my flies and asked me if I did anything with it or that sort of thing. I said, yes, I had been to bed with this other fellow at college. But again thinking of it now, of course, he set about it very awkwardly, indeed nothing came of this at all. I hadn't an erection, I was not interested, it was like a biologist looking at something under a microscope. I think this was when the actual consciousness of my homosexuality first appeared. I was at the University of Johannesburg, where a friend of mine gave me a book that he'd had from the library. It was a touching little tale, and it culminated in the disclosure that the dead young man had in point of fact been in love with another man. I realised then that, that was the sort of thing that could happen to me.

I think either my ability to suppress or repress physical sexual appetites as well as mental fantasies must have been very strong. So that I've always thought of myself as a late developer. But even what I've been saying, of course, is an indication that the development was there but I was able to control it, I controlled very well.

That particular friend, he and I were very, very good friends and we remained friends for years and years and years. In point of fact, in 1939 we took a flat together. Consequently, we both knew that the other was gay, but nothing was ever said, nothing at all. I think he too was in ignorance.

It was during my school teaching years that I really came into contact with homosexuality. There was a big drama festival held in Johannesburg to raise money for the university library, which had been burnt down. I was in one of the groups and I was taking part in the trial scene of *The Merchant of Venice*. There was a man who was in the company and he complimented me very much and said his sister had been so impressed with my voice, and so on and so on. Which of course pleased me. And he invited me to his flat one evening. The first thing he did when I arrived, which was not unnatural, was he offered me a drink. In those days I was still fairly young and was not a drinker. I didn't drink regularly at all. And so I had a gin and lime. For years afterwards the smell of gin and lime for me was the signal for a sexual experience. We had strawberries and then we sat on a sofa and he put his arm around me. Actually, if I remember rightly, we made very little actual love-making, but eventually he took me upstairs to his bedroom. I don't think we entirely undressed, but, in lying together, and I presume he was touching me, I ejaculated, to my intense embarrassment. I didn't know what one did under these circumstances. I said what do I do now? Which I recall infuriated him. Obviously he didn't understand the position I was in, and he felt that I was merely cutting off the whole affair, whereas I felt I was in a mess and I didn't know what to do. I don't think I ever went to his place again, probably because he didn't invite me. It might have been a very pleasant episode, but it was really one of just great embarrassment for me. I didn't look actively for other contacts afterwards.

I met a man, I think it was at a musical concert in Johannesburg. I don't know whether it was there and then that this man started to speak to me. But he then invited me to go for a picnic, and we went for a picnic and at some stage we had sex. It had an unfortunate consequence in that he must have instructed me and persuaded me to fuck him, because this was quite, quite beyond my experience altogether.

My total sexual experience was masturbation. As a result I got an infection which produced a discharge from the penis. I went to a doctor and to a specialist and I actually went to hospital. In those days they hadn't the drugs which could clear that up quickly, and I was put into hospital on a fat-free diet, which eventually cleared it up. Subsequently the specialist, who obviously felt nervous because I was already teaching one of his sons, gave me a talking to and said that what I was going in for was really immoral and unnatural and to be avoided at all costs. I had told him I got it from another man! I think probably that had an effect of putting me off having sex with somebody else for quite a long time. I was upset and worried that this could happen.

I remember during my university days thinking that a married life was not for me. That my job would be to look after my parents as they grew older. Which is an interesting rationalisation now, to think that I was heroically and consciously putting off married happiness in order to look after my parents, but really, what I was not realising, I was saying to myself, was that I didn't want to marry a woman anyway, you see. Incidentally, talking of women, all through my schooldays I was a great one for having a sweetheart and imagining that I was in love and writing love letters. And during my university days I was very friendly with a lovely, lovely girl, and you know we became partners and with a little group we went to dances and had tennis parties at her house. Very nice, very nice indeed. I think her mother would have fought tooth and nail against her marrying me, simply on the grounds that I was not nice enough or socially acceptable. However, of course, that faded out.

I tried twice to have sex with women. Once when I was away on holiday camping with another man, and we picked up two nice girls and they came to bed with us, but I was completely unsuccessful in doing whatever was required. Then, two or three years after, I was on holiday in Cape Town and the occasion was quite convenient, and had there been any desire on my part it could have been very pleasant, but I had no erection, and no sexual feelings. I had no physical feeling for a woman at all.

My ability to repress and to conceal was strong, although I must have been pretty effeminate, pretty homosexual in gesture and my voice and things of that nature. But there was no activity on my part which could endanger my position as a schoolteacher. Whether my feelings of guilt were causing me to suppress, under any pretext, my real homosexual nature, or whether I was really frightened at what could happen to me as a schoolteacher if I were revealed as a homosexual, I'm not sure. I imagine it was the first of those two, that I was fighting against surrendering to my homosexual nature.

In the years of my schoolteaching I had an affair with a fellow, I don't know where or how I met him. Might have been in some dramatic activity, and a couple of times I had sex with him, but that was all. And then I had a friendship for a short time with a fellow who quite obviously was a homosexual, but there was never any sex between us and no talk of homosexuality. At any time I wasn't conscious of being effeminate or camp. I was just a gay young thing. I was a very happy person. In fact, I think I've been extraordinarily lucky all my life, I've had a very happy life. I know it's easy now to forget unhappy periods. There was a period while I was at university when I was unhappy and that might have been partly sexual unfulfillment, but also I was aware of social inferiority to some of my university friends who had very fine homes and tennis courts and all that sort of thing.

But then I started teaching and I was at a boarding school. My very first job was in Pretoria. During the week of teaching I was quite happy, but when I went home to Johannesburg somehow I usually became depressed and melancholy. But that couldn't have lasted for long because then I started working in Johannesburg. I was always active. I was teaching, I was a boarding-house master, which meant there were duties there, and also by this time I had established myself as a radio actor, and also as a part-time radio announcer, so that I was always very busy. And quite happily so.

At one point in Johannesburg there was a so-called clean-up operation. There was a lot of talk going on, and various names of prominent people were mentioned. I think now some of them quite erroneously. I remember going to a party given by one of my schoolboys at his home. He was already seventeen or eighteen. It was a grown-up party, at the time of the clean-up operation, and this student of mine at some stage in the course of the evening made some remark jokingly implying that I might be in the cleaning-up operation. With some readiness I laughed and said, yes, me and the Bishop of Johannesburg. I don't think I was in any danger then of being cleaned up because I wasn't doing anything, at least I don't think so. Just this fellow I met a couple of times. Obviously all this time I was masturbating. But if you asked me what my fantasies were, I don't know. I can't remember.

My first 'relationship' was in the early days of the war, before I joined up. I was taking part in a play production, and one of the actors, whom we all disliked very much at first because he was so flamboyant and noisy, was the one who I fell for ultimately. I must have known that he was gay, he couldn't have been so flamboyant, I think, otherwise. And so we started going to bed together. Really that was my first experience of having a relationship with somebody, of thinking to myself that this was love. He was more experienced and wiser than I and he said that as soon as the run of that play was over, I would revert to being a respectable conventional schoolmaster, and he was right. When the play was over the glamour fell away and, although I remained very affectionately inclined to him, there was no question of a continuing love affair.

He knew about the homosexual world and where people met, which I wasn't aware of. He had been for years a professional actor, and there was no attempt on his part to conceal anything. I suppose everybody knew that he was a homosexual. And I presume, therefore, that when people saw my relationship with him they must have realised that this was the case with me as well. No one said anything. Except I had some theatrical people in my flat for drinks one evening, and one fellow said to me, I don't know quite how he expressed it, but something like, well, you're as queer as the rest. I don't think I coped with the situation very smartly. I probably just felt embarrassed and felt it was uncalled for on his part. But, you see that's interesting, if they were all gay, I was not conscious of it. I must have invited some and others came, and if they were all gay, as far as I was concerned it was accidental.

A woman friend of mine said to me once, you should read Edward Carpenter's *Love's Coming of Age*. I knew what she was getting at. For years I remembered that I should read Edward

Carpenter's book. And I never did. I have become aware only in, shall we say, the last two or three years of the magnificence of some of the Victorian militants in various fields. Up until then I had always thrown everybody into the category of the 'Victorians' and they were hateful and quite abominable and were guilty of such terrible repercussions right through the subsequent decades. But now my perspective is different and I have such admiration for Carpenter and Havelock Ellis and Olive Schreiner and some of the novelists of the period, for what they were doing.

When the war came, I got permission from the Education Department to join up. This was the early days of the war, 1940 or 1941, and I joined the South African Navy, which meant that I went a thousand miles away from home to Cape Town. From a previous theatrical visit to Cape Town, I knew a man there and that he was gay. So I renewed acquaintance and that really produced some very pleasant results. I had a slight affair with him for a while. Afterwards his home was always a home for me. He was quite marvellous and generous in his desire to do anything at all for people in the forces, and consequently I would go to his home, particularly on a Sunday lunch time when he would have quite a big lunch party, and they were all gay people. There I met quite a number of people and had affairs with them. All of which were very charming, in point of fact were very nice indeed. At perhaps the first of these gay parties I went to somebody used the word 'camp'. And I asked what it meant and of course this produced big laughter. Goodness me, my education really happened so late, because at this time I was already thirty-two.

After a time I went up the coast where I worked for a month, and then once a month we were supposed to have a long week-end in Cape Town. We contrived things, manipulating the watches, so that we could get off on Friday morning or Thursday.

I think because I was Commanding Officer, I felt that it would be lowering my own dignity and my own worthiness to hold that position if I were sexually free with any of the men on my station, so it was when I went to Cape Town that I had my sexual life. I didn't know of any bars in Cape Town, I don't think there were such things in those days. I was aware that the station was a meeting place, or a possible pick-up place then.

Come 1943 I came up to the Mediterranean. There it was very easy to pick up other servicemen. In Italy there was a little urinal which we frequented, and picked up people. One other thing which was very interesting and important in my life was that at a certain stage I was stationed in Rome. I was there for a couple of months. There was a civilian who somehow was attached to the South African forces. A very cultured Hollander. And he and I met quite normally, and after a time we realised that we were both gay. He introduced me to a little party, we went out to dinner one night and then back to an Italian army officer's flat and I realised, for the first time, that sexual relationships need not be furtive and come by chance and be transient. That in point of fact you could be with homosexual men and there might be no mention of sex whatsoever. There was this little group: an American, this Hollander, an Italian officer, a French press officer, and me. Most interesting people, cultured and intellectual. Up until then I had thought that homosexuality, or the indulgence in homosexual sex, was something between you, and, well, I hate to say so, but I suppose what I mean is, with inferior people. Not necessarily socially inferior, because during the war I was having affairs with sergeants of the army or air mechanics from the navy, and there was no social implications there. So that experience was an extremely valuable one. It opened up to my eyes the idea that there could be homosexual relationships with your equals and which could have, what seemed to me then, really an elevated nature.

I joined the Communist Party in December, in 1944, in London of all places. I say 'all places' because I was a South African, but I happened to be over here from Italy. I became interested in communism as an intellectual pursuit through the influence of another schoolmaster who had a tremendous intellect. He had a most wonderful mind, his mind was an encyclopedia, he really was tremendous. He had read and understood Marxism. Even though he was not ever a member of the Communist Party, or even active at all, but for him it was an intellectual fascination, and he dropped in casual remarks, which were Marxist tenets. To me they were absolutely eye-opening and shaking, because they were challenging to my normal conventional views. I think probably he lent me a couple of books and so my mind was developing for two or three years along the lines of communism.

What interests me very much is that it was at that very time that I was becoming painfully, almost unhappily, aware of my homosexuality. I think there is a possibility that my interest in communism was stimulated by my desire to be liberated from the oppression of my homosexuality. The Communist Party I recognised as a party which was working for liberation, of all sorts of liberation, but in particular South Africa, and liberation of the blacks. I think that unconsciously I was moving towards the Party in an expectation or a hope that I would find liberation from my sexual quandary.

So I became intellectually more and more interested in communism, until war broke out. The war certainly increased one's political awareness. I was ashamed at how politically igno-rant I was up until just before the war. So that for example, the persecution of the Jews in Germany was an item of news to me. I didn't go to protest meetings in Johannesburg. And, for instance, during the Spanish War, when I knew some people in South Africa had joined the International Brigade, there was never any thought on my part that I might be involved. I think, you know, that's pretty disgraceful, now.

With the coming of the war my political conscience became more pointed. I realised that I was going to be freed from the school by the Education Department to join up, and then I made contact with the Communist Party in Johannesburg and said I wanted to become a member. In those days you had to serve a probation, and somebody came to see me and gave me some books to read and I was to serve this probation period of six months. But before that expired I joined the navy. And so that put a close to my immediate contact with the Party. I still carried on the ideas and read more. When it came to the cele-bration of the October Revolution in Russia, I prepared a lecture and gave it to my own men on the station.

Then I went up to the Middle East. I was now ready and ripe to join, but it was while I was in London, at the end of 1944 that I had contact with some communists and one of them said, well you shouldn't go back to the Middle East until you've joined the party, so I joined in Britain. When I went back to South Africa I joined the Party again.

In the meantime, I had become a militant for a progressive ex-service organisation and, when I went back to South Africa, I resigned from school teaching and I started working for this organisation. Really that was my political assignment. I was a member of the Party and went to regular branch meetings, but my real work was in this broader field of ex-service affairs. We were a progressive organisation in that we had no colour bar, and that, of course, was unique in South African organisations, that there was no colour bar. Consequently, you know, we mounted a great campaign for the 1948 election in the hope that Smut's party would win, of course, and it did not.

My work went on in that organisation, which at a certain stage changed its nature and was no longer an ex-service organisation but we opened the ranks to whites in general. We formed the Congress of Democrats, which was the white organisation standing four square with the African National Congress, the Indian Congress and the Coloured People Congress. My work went on very actively. Then came September 1953, when the government banned me under the Suppression of Communism Act, which meant that I was out of work. I was also prohibited from speaking in public. I had become a fairly adept public speaker. So they shut me up.

In these intervening years I had started producing plays. After my professional acting experience my interest really was in producing, and I produced plays for the organisation, the ex-service organisation, to raise money. I chose plays with a social content and they were very successful, because the plays were good and because I had success as a director. Consequently, before I was banned, I was engaged by three professional companies to produce plays professionally. So, after looking for work after my banning, and not getting work because I was a banned person, I decided I would stand on my own feet professionally, as a producer of plays.

The Communist Party went underground and I was asked to join. I didn't know what to do. You are confronted with a situation and you think, oh God, I would rather opt out! Out of fear of some kind. And on this occasion when I was given the opportunity to rejoin the Party, part of me said, oh for Christ's sake, let me be, I don't want to get into any difficulties and so on. The question is what urged me forward, because I did join and I was a member of the Party until I left South Africa. I don't know whether I'm right in saying it, but all Party activity in South Africa was motivated primarily by the need to have liberation for the non-white people, and in so doing liberate the whites as well. Whereas in Britain, for example, economic factors are where you start. To me, race liberation was a part of my being, of my reason for being, it was absolutely overriding and compelling, so that I imagine that, in spite of my timidity, it was a conscious decision that this is a fight I must go on with. And I did.

My homosexual life continued to develop during this time. I had been having casual affairs, picking people up at a cottage, or meeting people elsewhere occasionally and having temporary affairs, but nothing lasting at all. Until I met a fellow somewhere about 1954. And, well, I fell in love with him. He was a difficult customer to be in love with. We established quite a relationship, we were a partnership, a couple, and it went along for quite a while, perhaps a couple of years. It was made easier by the fact that he worked and lived about twenty-five miles outside of Johannesburg. Therefore he only came over for the weekends, on Saturday afternoon he would come into the flat and we'd spend the weekend together. He was very independent and was very critical. When I introduced him to my family and friends, with never ever any talk of homosexuality, he usually disliked them and this made our weekends a little bit difficult because I would like to spend my weekends with my family and friends.

Then I came overseas in 1955, for a holiday which turned out to be a very nice working holiday. While I was away, still feeling very much in love with him, I had a letter from him saying that he'd met somebody else that he thought he could make his life with. This upset me very much and I cut short my holiday and went back. I simply laid down the law, I told him how foolish he was and that he didn't know when he was on to a good thing and he'd better reconsider, which he did. For a time. Then he came to work in Johannesburg and so he came and lived in my flat. But then there came a time when my mother died, and, well, I won't go into the whole business about that but, at that stage, this friend behaved quite abominably. He had no expression of sympathy or no consideration at all, and I told him that the affair was over and he must leave the flat. So that was the end of that.

I was not afraid of it being found out that I was living with someone. For a long time of course I thought that nobody else would think that I was homosexual. Then there came a time when I realised that my friends in the Party and friends outside the Party were sophisticated and that they would know exactly what was going on, but the interesting thing is that it was never mentioned. I didn't mention it and my friends didn't mention anything, in fact the topic of homosexuality was eschewed, probably out of delicacy for my feelings.

This was just a few years after the changes in the Soviet Union when Stalin made homosexuality illegal again, and in the western communist parties they were always talking about homosexuality as the bourgeois decadence. It makes me realise that the members of the Party at that time must have had considerable faith in me. Realising that I was a homosexual, they nevertheless put every trust in me. I never came into conflict with the police about my homosexuality, but it was a fear that they might catch me, not in some communist activity, but somehow or other on the homosexuality. That was a great fear. In later years I was happy enough to have sex relations with some black people as well as with whites. Previously, of course, it had been only with whites, there was no question of anything else. That made me nervous too because I thought, oh my heavens, they can expose me on so many counts now, of being a communist, of being a homosexual and, what's more, of having sex with black people.

I met the blacks through theatre work. In later years I was approached to run an acting course of workshops for a group of Africans. Out of that developed some of my most interesting and fulfilling work. I produced actual plays with these groups, and that went on right until I left South Africa, even though the Special Branch, the political police, were interfering and trying to stop this union of artists, a non-racial organisation which engaged me, to put on the plays with the blacks. They were intimidated, called down to the police headquarters and asked why they employed a well-known communist. But it went on and that was marvellous. It was in those circumstances that I met a few blacks, but also I can think of two other occasions when I met them casually.

One fellow whom I had sex with two or three times, in point of fact was having a relationship with a white man, which endured under those difficult conditions in South Africa, for years and years, twenty or thirty years. I learnt about it subsequently and I thought it was absolutely tremendous and marvellous. Even so that particular black man was married and has children.

In the full meaning of the word prostitution, as a real professional occupation, I would say at that stage there wasn't any. There were people who were known as rent, whom you could pick up. But then they would either demand money or threaten you in some way or other. That happened to me once. But I still don't think that it was a full-time occupation. They were white. At least I think of them only as white. Of course blacks were not allowed in the centre of Johannesburg after six o'clock in the evening. There was a complete curfew. So you walked the streets, and the only people you saw were white people, except black watchmen on buildings.

There were occasions, many occasions, and certain outstanding occasions when I thought, oh God, you know, can't you let me out of this political war? But of these particular special occasions I always made the right response. I came out I think on the right side. I'm not aware of going through life with a feeling of tension. I think any tension would be aroused by a particular situation. So that if, for example, I were driving a particular person, who probably the police were looking for, somewhere else, a journey of two or three hundred miles, then I would be under tension. Or if I knew that I was carrying banned literature in my car from A to B, then I'd be tense. But, I'm not aware of going through life being tense. In point of fact, it's one of the lucky things about my personality that I am a pretty gay creature, who's able to enjoy things and easily put behind me the causes of anxiety or distress.

In August of 1962 the police arrested me at the time when I was chauffeuring Nelson Mandela. They picked us up, and that was, of course, a terrible, terrible event. I am always sorry that it was while I was driving Nelson that he was picked up, because from that day to this he has remained in prison, and he is in prison for the rest of his life.[1] It was two years after Sharpeville and we were inside prison. I was inside for three months then.

After that I thought it's about time I came overseas again. I hadn't made an attempt to get away before that for two reasons. Number one, I no longer had a passport, the South African police had taken my passport away and, secondly, I had fallen, to my surprise, in love again. That happened in 1959. This was four or five years after my first episode, and by that time I was over fifty. I wasn't breaking my heart about it but I thought well, my days of love were over. And then I fell in love, and I think this proved to be the one great love of my life. In fact obviously I have not fallen in love very often, but this one was. So for two reasons I was being held in South Africa. But now, I thought I should make use of my British birth, and I got a British passport. I began to think maybe I should get out before next spring [1963], because, well, something may happen to me, they may pick me up for some reason or other.

While I was thinking like this I was served with a summons to answer questions about the earlier charge, which I refused to do. I had a lawyer with me. First of all the prosecuting side said that the penalty for not answering questions was eight days in prison, and then I would be brought back and given again the opportunity to answer questions and be taken back and forth as long as they liked. My lawyer said that's nonsense, this was not a criminal offence and so the magistrate finally said okay, I could be released at my own recognisance, but that I must surrender my passport. I said, oh well, the police already have my passport, which was quite true about the South African passport. That again made me think, I must go soon, otherwise I'll lose this opportunity altogether. I started enquiring about air fares and the places that I would like to visit on my way to Britain. Then there came a night when they came, the police came, and they put me under house arrest. I was allowed out during the day, but I had to be in my flat from six o'clock in an evening till half-past-six the next morning and throughout the weekend and had to report to the police every day, somewhere between twelve and two, and I was not allowed to leave the magisterial district of Johannesburg.

After they had served me with these papers I got back in bed and I decided, I am going to get out. Things were very lucky, I have always been a very lucky person, because the next morning in the paper there was a report that various people had been put under house arrest, but my name was not there because, when they had come to my flat earlier in the evening, I was out. So they had to come back after midnight and I missed the morning papers. That gave me that morning, Saturday morning. I went back madly between the bank and the building society and the air agent, and I ended up at eleven o'clock with an air ticket made out to various places in Europe, and I had £800 in travellers' cheques. At midday the placards came out announcing that a theatre director was under house arrest. If that had happened in the morning I couldn't have got my travellers' cheques or air tickets, so it was lucky. It took me ten days to organise it but I did. I was driven over the border into Botswana, and from there I made my way up.

I didn't ask the Party for help. I didn't ask anybody. The only help came in two directions. Most important was finding the suitable person to drive me out to the border and then I could just walk over the border. It would have been lunatic for me to ask any of the known communists because their movements were probably being watched even more closely than mine. I had to consider the circumstances of the individual, so that, for instance, a man who might have helped me, or a woman who might have helped me, I wouldn't ask, because if she became known then her husband could, for example, lose government contracts. I couldn't ask such and such a fellow because he was working for the telegraph department, I couldn't ask so and so's mother who has got a weak heart or is an invalid, etc. ... But eventually it all worked out very well and the particular fellow, a friend of mine, said he would do anything he could.

I worked out which direction to go, because I wanted to go in a direction I could get to Swaziland or Botswana, but I also wanted to go in the night time because the police had twice come to my flat to check that I was there at certain times, and they searched my flat to see there was nobody visiting me, because no one was allowed there. I knew that I was pretty safe in the middle of the night. I wanted to ensure there would be time for that fellow to get back into Johannesburg before the police knew I was away. They would know by two o'clock in the afternoon when I failed to report to the police station. So this fellow helped me immeasurably in this way.

Another fellow who was a liberal, he was a gay fellow—I think he thought of me as being something of a political hero—he had said to me, if ever you want to escape, he had a friend near the border who knew a hidden route across the border. I got in touch with him, and asked him to contact his friend. In point of fact, I didn't make use of that route. But he was ready to help me.

I got to Botswana early in the morning. My friend dropped me at the border and then I had to wait there until dawn. Eventually a little pick-up van came through with a farmer who was so taciturn that we didn't exchange a single word, I just said, will you give me a lift and he did. Then I was merely concerned with getting away up to Salisbury or Bulawayo. It was very interesting. I went to the police commandant—a British force occupied Bechuanaland in those days—and I told him who I was and I said I expected his protection against any possible gang of South Africans coming over the border to abduct me, which had happened, on two or three occasions, to other people in other places. He said, go and have a chat with his security men and, while I was chatting, the commandant came back and said, well news travels fast. He'd just had a call from the

Johannesburg radio station to confirm that I was there. And he told me that he had said he'd never heard of me.

It's very interesting how that information had got back so quickly. By about half-past-eleven the hotel proprietor, where I had booked in, had recognised me, and he had sent word through, because he was also the local correspondent for the evening paper. I booked on a plane, which was then flying to Nairobi and that's as far as I wanted to go then, because I wanted to go to Cairo. So I got on this plane which was half empty, and the hostess brought me that afternoon's Johannesburg *Star*. I looked through it, and in the centre page there was a bloody great photograph of me, and an awful photograph too, which had been taken at one of these press interviews. So I thought, oh my God, now the hostess will recognise me and will report to the captain of the plane who will think it is his duty to turn back— it was a South African airways plane. Everybody afterwards said I must have been mad in any case to go on a South African plane, but anyway nothing happened.

When I arrived back in England I went straight to Glasgow. I wanted to take a television production course, and I discovered that the place where I would be likely to get such a course was in Glasgow, and not with the BBC who were more concerned with training people from their own ranks. So I went to Glasgow, and in fact stayed there for eight years.

My lover had come back to Britain in the meantime after I left South Africa, to finish his doctorate. So we just set up house together. It worked out quite well. I only got involved in the gay scene very slightly. We had an introduction to a couple of fellows, and we introduced ourselves, and invited them to come to dinner at our flat, and through them we met two or three others, but we only had this very limited acquaintance. We invited many people to dinner and they were delighted to come, the evenings passed very pleasantly, but year after year passed and nobody invited us back to their homes. After eight years I hardly knew anyone in Glasgow.

When I moved down to London I found it a marvellously friendly place, even officials. I have found that making friends here is very much easier. I have a great number of gay friends and they visit me and I visit them. We go to a theatre together or something. Of course, I also have a number of married friends. Quite a number of whom are South Africans, you know, links with the past.

But to this day, I find it difficult to discuss my homosexuality with straight people. I have really only referred to my homosexuality explicitly at the beginning of last year [1977] when we split. Even then, without using the word 'homosexual', of course, it was not necessary for some friends. I would say, well you know we have split up. Their reaction was very friendly and warm, of sympathy. Exactly as if they were talking to two heterosexual people who've split up. Similarly I told my brother and his wife that we have split up. They were very sorry. They've always known, in other words. I think I am readier now if an occasion should arise, to say, yes, I am gay. But I don't make an occasion. I have one lesbian friend now who had been a friend of mine for, I should think, getting on for thirty years. It was not until twenty years ago that we both met at a gay party and we found we were both gay. She's now in Britain. I am very great friends with her and her partner. I'm very relaxed and enjoy myself in lesbian compan, but, come to think of it, I know very few who visit me or whom I visit often.

I think attitudes to homosexuality have changed quite marvellously, in point of fact. I have not done anything in the campaigns for gay liberation or for the Campaign for Homosexual Equality personally. Yet I have the greatest admiration for the people who have run these organisations and who run whatever organisations are still being run and gratitude for them to. I've just been in Spain. And I imagine that under Franco homosexuality was absolutely banned. I don't know whether the law has been changed but I was tremendously impressed when I saw posters advertising a gay congress which took place a couple of weeks before I was there. I saw that in two cities. In Zaragoza and in Barcelona. Such movement towards liberation in a country like Spain could not have jumped up so quickly and so suddenly and so strongly, had it not been prepared by the movements in other European countries. And I think it's a great thing.

It is shameful that in the socialist countries it is still a crime. To me it's a negation of the whole liberatory process of socialism and communism that there should be this violent suppression of homosexuality. I had quite accepted myself as a homosexual as far as that first love affair I had in 1954. I don't say that I'd reached the stage where I was ready to go out and wear a badge, not in those years. But I was completely able to accept myself as a homosexual. Then, certainly when I fell in love for the second time, and that was so deep and lasted so long, I felt my personality was integrated. The only difference I feel now is that, if the occasion should arise, and it would depend on circumstances, I still am not going to say to any Tom, Dick or Harry that I am homosexual, but with an interested third party, and where there would be some point to it, well then, you know, I am prepared to say that I am gay.

Note

1. Nelson Mandela was finally released in February 1990.

10 A dancer's life

Sam was born in 1910 in Cambridge. As a young boy he contracted an illness which left him with a slight limp for the rest of his life. Despite this handicap, he became a dance instructor, and for a time ran his own school in Cambridge, where he lived with his mother. He had in fact left school at fourteen, and been apprenticed to the soft furniture trade. This became the main source of his livelihood throughout his life and, when he was interviewed, it still supplemented his pension. After leaving Cambridge after the Second World War and the death of his mother, he lived in London and then the Medway towns before retiring to the south coast, where he became active in a local gay group. In this interview he concentrates on his sexual life, and in particular on his involvement with predominantly heterosexual men.

When I lived in Cambridge I used to have a dancing school and, after the war broke out, I got a show together and used to go round the aerodromes. We had a lot of young aerodromes made specially for the Yanks when they came over into the war, and we used to go out entertaining them. I've been on the boards myself professionally and I used to take a show around. I produced it out of my own pupils from the school. I had three girls and three boys on the staff, as well as my dancing partner. If there was a ball on in Cambridge, they'd have us to demonstrate and I used to take my three girls and three boys, and used to dress them alike so that they did formation dancing.

I used to like a bit of fun, I mean I used to have fun when I was a boy in the choir, with one or two of the choirmen who used to run after me. But I never thought it was anything. I thought it was just being adolescent, a sort of phase and I would sort of grow out of it. As a matter of fact, I used to knock around with one or two girls during that time. But I never had sex with them, it was merely being with them, kissing them. I think I was getting on for twenty when I suddenly realised. I saw ballets and things like that and I wondered why I was more attracted to the male form than the woman's form.

I met one or two people in the town that were gay, but I didn't actually know it, and when I explained to one of them that, you know, this happened when I went to see ballet and that kind of theatre he just smiled at me and says, yes, I thought so, you're queer, you see. So I said, oh that's it, is it? He took me down to where the pub was, where they all met. At that particular time we had a pub in Cambridge called the 'Still and Sugarloaf'. It ran underneath the cinema and it was called the Long Bar. There was no women allowed down there, it was all male, you see, so of course it was quite a good place. They weren't allowed to have women in there, not to serve even. Of course, one or two of the men were gay too and the manager was a nice chap, although he wasn't, he knew all about it. He knew us all and called us all by name. Very nice chap he was. We used to get together down there, especially Saturday nights. It was very nice, although it was behind locked doors. It was more exciting because you could get away with that kind of thing.

I used to sometimes give tea dances on a Sunday afternoon, at the studio, or perhaps a drag show. As a matter of fact my parties got quite well known and they used to come down from London. They used to call me Lady May Cambridge. They said Lady May's putting on another do, and they all used to come down. Of course we had a wonderful time. We used to put on shows for ourselves and one or two of the pupils. A lot of my pupils knew, you know, and some very nice boys I had that used to enter in the fun. I had lots of my pupils too, boy pupils. If I made a play for them they thought it was wonderful to be loved by a Principal at the school of dancing. I always used to 'do' them of course.

I should think right up till when I was thirty, I always done the boys. And I had quite a lot of them. And some of them very nice too, lovely boys. And then I turned over to the other way round. Yes, looking back, soldiers, sailors and airmen couldn't expect them to let me do them, although some of them didn't mind, I'm sure. But it was usually the other way around and I met, oh, ever so many of them. Of course, during the war, apart from the fact that it was horrible to know why it was caused, it was really intriguing because you wondered who you was going to meet in the blackout. You got a lot of straight men. I used to go up to London with my affairs for the weekend, and we used to go to the theatre and that. Two gay friends of mine who were having an affair, and my affair at the time, we used to come up and stay in hotels. When you booked in and you just said double rooms, they didn't turn a hair. If it was for two men or two females, it didn't matter to them. After the war it got a bit more stricter. But during the war, of course, a lot of people left London, so London was pleased for anyone who came up to take bed and breakfast.

I was living in a good part of Cambridge. It was a very nice road where you weren't far from the centre of town. Behind our street was a great big car park where lorry drivers used to come and park. I used to look round to see if any of them weren't asleep, because the driver used to sleep in the cab. I used to say would you like to come and sleep at mine? I used to get ever so nice chaps, awfully nice. Of course, all of them married.

The point was that during that time you never knew whether you were going to be here today and gone tomorrow. They all had that attitude that they just lived for the day, and they couldn't care less.

There were all these aerodromes around from where the Yanks used to come into Cambridge, because that was the nearest city for them. They used to be brought in on their lorries, and then all taken back at night. Of course, if you walked about after the pub closed about 11 p.m. you found one or two where they'd missed the lorry and, if you thought they were nice, you just invited them back for the night. I was living in a house then and we took in lodgers you see, because it was a ten-roomed house, and I only had my mother. My two brothers were in the forces.

There was only me and my mother at home. I was always taking people home. She never queried anything, as a matter of fact she knew. I didn't tell her. Well, she must have guessed, I never took any girls home. A friend of hers met her in the street, she said, I see your Sam never leaves you, she said, he's always with you and he never seems to be with a girl or want to get married. She said, no, he's not made that way. That's all she said. And this woman told me about the conversation.

Of course, all my friends, personal friends knew and I think lots of them had an idea. My dancing partner knew and all my staff knew. During and after the war they hadn't got the same prejudice that they had before the war. I mean you couldn't even let anyone know, not even the next-door neighbour, that you were gay before the war. Or that you practised anything. They might call you queer, but probably only because of the way you talked, but they wouldn't think anything about sexually. They'd call you queer because they thought you was a bit girlish. But not because of the sexual act.

I remember at school there was one boy there, you always get one in school who is a bit bossy, and they called him school bully. He was always bossy and he always picked on the smallest and weakest to intimidate, and he used to pick up on me because I was lame and sort of a weakling. He used to call me Lizzie. Only because he thought of me as a girl. I was more effeminate-looking than the other boys. I was brought up different too, I was brought up to speak politely, whereas these other boys who were like him, from the East End of London, were more common. The women often used to say to me, if I met them in a pub and there was a nice boy, What about him Sam, you like him? and all that. Often I used to think, yes, a very nice one too! Lovely people. They were quite sincere. As a matter of fact, one of the girls, if she heard anyone saying anything against me, she'd go for 'em. Oh yes. Oh yes. She was a vicious little thing for that! Mind she was a beautiful girl, a lovely nature but, oh, she couldn't half lash out with her tongue if she heard anything against me. No, they were all lovely girls I had there.

I wondered if my being gay would pass off. I wondered if it was a thing that everyone went through. And then I found that

I was having love affairs. I began to fall in love, not with the boys, of course, because they were just for sex. My first affair was during the war. I met an English airman. He was just standing on his own and he looked so sorrowful that I spoke to him. He was quite pleased to speak to me and I found out he'd been transferred to an RAF base just outside Cambridge and he turned out to be Welsh, a Welsh boy from Pontypool, and he hadn't been married long. His wife was expecting their first baby. I think it must have been in him but dormant because, as soon as he met me, he realised and we had a marvellous affair while he was in Cambridge. So much so that if he couldn't get out from his camp he used to ring me and talk to me on the phone, and then when he was posted away for a little while he used to ring me and write to me every day. In one of his letters he said, 'I don't know how to explain it', he says, 'but I'm so wrapped up in you I don't know whether I'm coming or going'. Then he went abroad. I saw him once or twice when he came back. But we didn't carry on so violently like that and as things had altered during the war while he was away, all sorts of people had emerged, and I'd had other affairs. They all sort of drifted back to their own homes after the war, but while they were there, they were very nice.

I've had very nice affairs with soldiers. I was somewhere for them to come to get away from the barracks. I was also their drinking friend, because they didn't get much money and I always had plenty, so I used to look after them well and my mother always used to treat them as though they were at home. They always had their meals with me, home cooking.

It was funny. I was walking home one day and before you reach my house there was a big common. They used to have a fair on there, and partly during the year we used it for grazing cows and horses. It used to be a place that if soldiers missed their bus, they'd probably go just inside and lay under a tree, if it was warm. This particular night I was coming along and there was a little soldier, he was only about five feet three or four. He was sitting on the railings. It was very hot and he'd got his shirt all open down to his belly button. He was sitting there, so I just walked along and I said, Hello, I said, you've missed your bus?

He said, yes. So I said, oh, I said, people are forever doing that. So he laughed. I said, you got nowhere to go? He says, no. So I said, it's a good job it's warm then isn't it? So he said, yes, it is. Well he'd got the hair down here you see, so I said, does that reach the other part? And he says, why don't you put your hand down and see? So I said, oh, all right, you can come back with me, and my God, what a cock he'd got! I've never seen anything like it in my life and he was ever so small in stature. So of course I said, what size shoes do you take? So he says, six. So I said, don't they pinch you? He laughed, he knew why, because you're supposed to have big feet if you have a big cock, you know. It was amazing, never seen anything like it in my life.

The point with these people was, when they went back to barracks they never knew whether there's an order to say you're moving. You could see them one day and the next time they just didn't turn up, they weren't there. So they had to make hay while the sun shines, the same as you. But once they'd met you and they knew they'd got somewhere to come to, they'd come and sleep with you as long as they could. Of course, when they'd gone away I used to have some lovely letters from some of them, wish I was still with you, or wish you were here, or something to that effect. I had lovely letters.

There's a terrible lot of my friends who were camp. I mean you'd only got to take one look at them and they'd probably come up. I used to have one friend who used to approach someone and say, 'Have you got a light, dear?' And then bring his knee up into their crutch! But I mean I never did. Of course, a lot of my affairs were very glad I was discreet because they could always be seen by other people with me, you see.

One night I was coming home again and I saw this Scotch boy, he was sitting on the grass leaning up against a tree. I knew he was Scotch because he was wearing a Glen Garry hat. I said to him, have you missed your bus? So he said, yes. I didn't quite press the idea at the particular time. Anyway, he looked quite nice. He was Alec, I can still remember his name, Alec, he was fair, very fair. Most of the Scotch didn't want any diagrams, they're the most susceptible people I've ever come across actually. Yes, Scotchmen are. Anyway, I thought I wouldn't press the idea, so I said to him, all right, I said, I only live two doors away along here. If you like, I said, come in and have some breakfast and clean yourself up. I hadn't thought no more about it. I went home. I thought, oh he won't follow. Anyway, about eight o'clock there was a knock on my back door. I wondered who the devil it was. So, oh, I said, that must be Alec. I said, I found a soldier, mum, lying under a tree, and I said to him come round have a wash and brush up and something to eat, and she said, oh, she said, oh well ask him in. So, of course, he was there and he came in.

My mother took to him straight away. He was a very nice boy. We spent the day together and then we went out to the pub. During the evening I said to him, have you got to go back? He said, oh no, he says. I'm staying for a week or so. So I said, well, would you like to stop with me? He said, oh yes. Very much, he said. From then on, of course, it was easy going. He told me about a pal of his called Tony. Now he used to talk about this pal of his, there was three of them. One called Tony, another one called Sailor. They called him Sailor because before he joined the army he was in the navy. They were all in the HLI [Highland Light Infantry], the tough lot of the Scotch regiments. Tough they were.

Well, about a week had gone by and I was going to the pictures that night. When I came home my mother met me at the door and she said, there's a friend of Alec's here to see you, called Tony. And when I went in and saw him, he was as handsome, oh my God, he was the handsomest kid. And, when he sat down, in his trousers it was sticking out there. Bloody great packet he'd got. And he smiled at me. He stayed for about ten days. And then I said goodbye to him, and a few more days had gone by and I was coming home again. Right on the corner of the common there was a toilet, a ladies' and gents' toilet. And I thought, oh I don't think I can wait until I get home, I'll have to call in there to have a pee. And just as I was going through the railings, out come a soldier with a Glen Garry on. And he looked at me, so I smiled back at him, and I said, HLI? So he said, yes. I said, you don't happen to know a chap called Alec? He said, are you Sam? He said, I'm Sailor. I felt, well I'll be blowed, here we go again. He was a tough bugger he was, oh really lovely he was. And they were all as gentle as anything. They made love to you, I mean they would do that, because they saw you as a woman really. That was the impression I got and also the way they performed. You can always tell you see.

I was out once with another friend of mine and we were going across another park into the centre of town and my friend says to me, look at those two soldiers over there, they're Canadians. So my friend said to me, come on, she says, we'll try and get these two. He was the one who used to go up with the cigarette and say, have you got a light, dear? I said, oh you'll get your bloody head knocked off, if you're not careful. I said, they're not even English. Oh, he said, that don't matter. She said, they are all alike. Anyway, she goes up and she said, Have you got a light, dear? You see to one of them. So of course they caught on. One of them was only eighteen, he was called Buddy. Oh, he was a handsome kid. They both were blond, the other one was a married man but not much older, he was about twenty-one or twenty-two. Anyway, we said, what are you doing? So they said, nothing, just killing time. So I said, come and have a drink. They said, yes, love to.

We took them in a pub and we sorted each one out with Buddy, sat on Buddy's side and my other friend sat on the married man's side. We got talking and, by the time the pub closed, they knew what it was all about. So of course I said, what are you two doing now, have you got anywhere to stay? They said, no, we'll stay out. I said, oh no you won't, come back with me if you like. So they said, both of us? I said, yes, certainly, I've got a large place. There's only my mother there.

They all came back. We were in the lounge there, all four of us and Buddy says, is there any other room where we could go to? So I said, I've got the attic upstairs. I said, you can go up there if you like. So I left my friend with this other soldier down in the sitting-room. We went up there, I could hardly get me damned trousers down before he was up me standing there! I had to lean against the wall. Oh poor bugger, he didn't half want it bad. And so anyway it was all over in oh, a few seconds, you know. And, oh he was beautiful, really beautiful and, when we went downstairs, my friend looked at me and he sort of laughed and he said, my God, that was quick! So I said, yes, it was. I said, I think if he hadn't had it he'd have done it in his trousers! We weren't down twenty minutes before he said, can we go upstairs again? Oh, I said, what? So he said, oh yes, he said, I could have done it there and then, he says. So of course, I said, all right, come on, I said, there won't be any peace until you do! They stayed at mine for somewhere around a fortnight. His cock was just like it had been taken out of cellophane! The head of it was real pink as though it had never been used before! Well, I don't suppose it had really. Although he didn't want any telling. He knew what to do. But he was only active. Oh yes, yes, definitely. He'd make love to you. And he didn't mind me playing with it and kissing it and all that kind of thing, he loved all that.

We got to the time when the war had gone on quite a bit and we had the prisoners of war. They were put in all the camps just outside Cambridge, and of course the first lot were the Italians, and they used to be allowed out into the street wearing green uniforms with patches on.

Well, first one'd come and then he'd probably bring his friend in the camp and before you know where you are you've got about half a dozen visiting you. They was crafty buggers! They used to go back to the camp and then dodge out in front of one another so they were first at mine, so they could have a bit of sex before the others arrived. I used to laugh like the devil to see how they used to work it you see. They'd got quite a way to go and they'd got to walk and they used to come in all out of breath because they walked to get there before the others. When they went back you know, they used to write to me. Used to have some lovely letters from them.

I was going up towards the camp one night with a friend of mine, and two German boys were fooling about in the street. Of course, lots of those were blond, because they were Aryan. They were captured early which they were very pleased of. Joachim said to me, as soon as we saw the British come we all put our guns down and put our hands up in the air. He was in the Panza division. A lot of those boys didn't want to go to war at all. They were calling them up as young as sixteen. It was getting so short of gun fodder and Hitler had to call them up. Joachim was only just turned eighteen, and he'd been in the war two years.

Well Johnny, Joachim, used to come to mine quite a lot and ring me up. Nothing happened for quite some time, we used to see one another, he used to come home with me. My mother was dead by then. He rang me up one day, in the afternoon. I'd finished teaching, I'd had a private dancing lesson. He says, are you alone Sam? I said, yes, do you want to come over? He said, yes. And of course he came over and it all happened. He'd fell in love with me and as he said, he'd had no sex for ages and ages and ages, and from then on we had a violent affair.

After a while I said, are you allowed out for weekends? So he said, yes, with the commandant's permission. And I said, are you allowed to wear civilian clothes? So he said, yes, if we're out. So I rang the commandant and I gave a name and address and I said he's been visiting me for some time, I'm actually a relation of his, I said, I'm a distant cousin, and he's been doing little jobs in the garden (because they were allowed to do that you see, had their own bit of money, pocket money). And I said, I was wondering, commandant, if it was all right for him to come out for a weekend, and also wear civilian clothes? He said, oh quite all right, quite all right. All you've got to do is to let me know when you want him to come and I'll sign a pass for him. And he said he's at liberty to wear ordinary clothes while he's with you. And I said, is it okay for him to go to London with me at any time? Oh yes, he said, certainly. And all I had to do was just ring him and say is it all right for him to have the weekend with me and we'll be going to London.

It came to the time, of course, of him having to go back to Germany and, oh dear, he cried and didn't want to go and all this, that and the other. But, of course, he'd got to. I gave him an old gramophone to take with him and one or two records. While he was in the prisoner-of-war camp he learnt English and, by the time he met me, he could speak it fluently and also write it. He hadn't been back about two or three days before he wrote me. He found his people were in the eastern zone, so he couldn't go back to them. He had to stay in Hanover.

We wrote to one another for months, and then he said he'd like to come over for a holiday. He got a passport and was allowed to come in the country for three months. He came over and stayed with me and he got a little extension. He hung on right till the last minute then he went back again.

He kept writing to me, and he said, 'Would you come over and see me?' you see. So I said, all right, and I went out there to see him. And oh, Germany was terrible. It was still a dilapidated affair. I was over there about a fortnight. He'd got in tow with a girl in his digs. The woman who took him in had got a daughter and she'd got a little baby. It wasn't his.

I didn't know this until I got there, and I found out that there was something between them, although he didn't want me to know it. So I went home. About three or four weeks later I had a letter from him, he said, you were quite right. It didn't work out. Can I come to England to be with you? I didn't write back. I ignored it. I thought it was best to leave it. I wasn't really upset because it had got to a point whereby I knew what was happening and I thought the same could happen again. He could find someone and do that kind of thing. So that was the end of that. But he was very charming, I liked him very much. We had a lovely time together.

After the war I had another sailor, he was married, got two children, I was godfather to the second one. While his wife was pregnant I used to go to the house and cook the meals for them. She knew that I was gay. She'd be more upset if it was a woman. She didn't see me as a threat. He used to drive me all about all over the place and be away for days when I first met him, and he wanted to be with me. Christ he'd got a cock too!

They'd got two children and she was pregnant with a third. The kids always used to call me Uncle Sam when I went there. Before that, he used to get away with an excuse. He used to say, I wanted someone to drive me, as I was lame, had a bad leg. He told her it would involve probably weekends and several evenings and she didn't mind a bit because it was pocket money for him as he said, see. And that's how he got away with it. I began to go home with him and her and the kiddies. I used to spend quite a lot of time there and then eventually she was due

to have her baby. She had it at home. I said to him, well I may as
well come home and look after you lot, while she's up there. He
said, would you? I said, yes, certainly.

I always thought if you were too masculine, especially if you
were in bed with them, that would probably put them off. So,
although I kept myself on the masculine side, if I was out with
them during the day or in a pub, when we were at home alone,
or in bed, I'd sort of switch on the femininity a bit for them. I
found that they accepted that.

I didn't resent it because I knew it was just for the purpose of
getting the atmosphere. I found I didn't want sex with any gay
person. I got to the pitch whereby I couldn't have sex with any
gay person. All my lovers were either bisexual or married or had
gone out with girls and done them. I couldn't have any sex with
anyone who was camp. That was most peculiar.

And if I was 'doing' anybody it had got to be a youngster.
That was another thing I had. Mind you, one or two of them I
done was just because they wanted me to, they just asked me to
do them, I suppose they wanted to find out what it was like. But
I mean it wasn't a thing that I pursued. But if I had a youngster,
I mean, I'd always be the male. I expected it, and they'd got to
expect it to, otherwise they're no good to me.

Smithy was another married man I knew. He used to like me
more than he did his wife. Used to go home to Scotland, put her
in the family way and then come back and see me. If he got on
her nerves, she used to say, go on back to London and see Sam.
Get out of it. In the end Smithy said to me, I wish I'd met you
before I married her, I wouldn't have married.

At the moment I'm having an affair with a married man,
Campbell, who lives a long way away. He was down last weekend actually. He's married with three children. I was having an
affair with him before he got married. He's been with me for
twelve, thirteen years now.

He hadn't got married when he met me. He met me through
Smithy. Smithy said any time you're in London, I was then living
in London, go and see Sam, he'll put you up. He said, of course
he's gay. Well this boy Campbell was nineteen then. He'd been
quite a flighty type. He'd come down from Scotland when he

was sixteen, and he knew a bit about it and, of course, being about in London he found he was doing everything and everyone he met. Mostly women. Occasionally he'd want a bed for the night and he'd go home with them if he met someone who obliged.

When he met me he said, I met Smithy and he told me to look you up when I was in London. I knew this Smithy had put him right. The first night Campbell and I went to bed, I said, goodnight. He was sleeping in my bed. I could see he didn't know what to do. He kept twisting and turning. I said, what's the matter? Oh, he said, it's being with you. So of course when I put my hand there he'd got a hard-on. I said, oh I suppose you want it do you? So he said, yes please. From then on it was every bloody night for a long while. We had an affair on and off for some time. Sometimes he'd get a bit fed up and go off somewhere and then he'd come back.

Eventually I moved out of London. I got a shop in the Medway towns. One day when I hadn't seen Campbell for some time, he said I'm ringing you from Gravesend. I said, oh you're back there are you? I knew he'd been seeing a bird somewhere round there. So I said, what, are you seeing this bird? He said, not only that, he said I've married her! Well, I said, you're a bit of a fool. Had he been with me, of course, I would have talked him out of it. I said, you didn't ask me to the wedding. He said, I couldn't, be too embarrassing. I couldn't have gone through with it if you'd stood there. Anyway, he said, it's not going to make the slightest bit of difference between us.

At that particular time they were living quite near me so he used to pop in every now and again. He'd leave off early at work and then come in to see me, then go on home. We used to see quite a bit of one another. Then I got to knowing her and the children. They used to call me Uncle Sam. She's jealous of me because she knows what I stand for and what I can give him. She's jealous when he comes to see me because she knows that when he comes here he has a good time. But she doesn't know anything about the sex. In fact it is his friend that he was at school with and used to be with in London for a long while, who he's known all his life, who she suspects of being the other lover! And yet they've never had sex, it's funny isn't it? I haven't seen his last child, a boy. And I haven't been down since I've been here. I used to see him a lot when I was in Medway because they lived quite near. They had these two girls.

He does still come down, he was here for four days. He's getting so fed up now, he's got his work, and she don't half lead him a life. You know what? She knew he wanted to come out one day, on a Saturday, he promised to come here. She knew he was coming out to see me and she got up early that morning, took the two girls and said I'm just going out, I'll take the two girls and I'll be back in half-an-hour. She left the boy behind you see. And that bugger went off for the day so he couldn't move. Yes. Went over to her mother who lives in Gravesend and left the baby there so he couldn't go out.

I was very pleased when I came to the south coast and found the CHE was here because I never knew anything about this at all. I never knew there was such a thing as the *Gay News*. And the whole time I was in Tunbridge Wells, I was there three years, and I never knew a soul there who was gay and I never knew about their place they'd got there. I found out because someone who was gay came to see me and they said, do you know there's a CHE here? And I said no, I didn't. So he said, I know the secretary, I'll get in touch with him and tell him to contact you. He said they meet twice a week. I said, well if you're going, take me with you, because I didn't want to go on my own. So he said, right I'll ring the secretary and tell him. He said, he'll pick you up in the car and told me what his name was. He took me in to where they had got a room over a pub. We all went in the bar first, which breaks the ice, and the secretary introduces you all round, to the convener, and everybody and they're all so nice. When you get in the room they say, first of all let us welcome a new member to the meeting. From then on it's very nice. Of course, they all come here to my house, I have an open night once a month, and they all come here. I've got a bring-and-buy coming up before I go to Benidorm. Then we have a raffle and, of course, that's how we get a lot of our money. In the summer we get a small minibus and go out to places for picnics, to places like Kew Gardens, Hampton Court. And then we also have discos. We hire the hall and do all our own catering. About a hundred or so come from all around. We get them from Hastings and Brighton and from the Medway towns. We get them from as far as Tunbridge Wells. Of course, we make quite a bit of money from those. I'm on the committee now.

I've enjoyed life much more since I joined CHE. They're always ringing me up and you're never alone, as you were before. Friday nights we've got a gay pub here where we all go to if we want to. That's where I took Campbell only last Friday and, of course, they all wanted to know who he was and the landlady behind there said, who's this lovely new man you've brought in, Sam? He blushed a bit but he falls in with it all. Of course, they all fall over him and it is wonderful really how he takes it.

11 A public servant's life

Stephen was born in 1910 into a middle-class family. He started his career in the Foreign Service and spent a tour of duty in Paris. He returned to England in 1934 and, partly because of his sexuality, transferred to the Home Civil Service in 1937 where he thought it would be easier to pursue his career. Stephen met his life-long partner just after the Second World War and they lived together for over thirty years, very much a 'married' couple.

I think my homosexuality goes back to school. I was at public school and, like many people at public school, I met various people I was desperately attracted to. But I must say nothing much actually happened. Well, then I left school and was working in London and didn't really take much part in the gay scene at that time and didn't know much about it. I had one or two friends, fortunately, one could talk to about it. There was one person I had quite a little affair with. This was when I was about nineteen, I suppose.

Well, then I passed into the Foreign Service and was posted to Paris and hadn't been there more than a week or so when the Consul General gave a party, an enormous mixed party, of course. An incredibly handsome young man appeared at this party and I was absolutely overwhelmed. In fact he and I, much to the annoyance of Mrs Consul General, spent the whole party sitting on the stairs talking to each other.

I had a year in Paris and during this time this young man was around and naturally we saw a good deal of each other. He was a student at the Sorbonne and when he left I was somewhat shattered. Subsequently, he wrote to me and said he was getting married. I hadn't really sort of reckoned on bisexuals in those days.

I had a little flat in Paris and this young man, with whom I was very, very deeply in love, would visit me. Looking back, I can't think what things one went through. After evenings in my flat he would never allow me to pay for a taxi for him to go home, because he was too proud and thought to take money would be unsuitable. So I used to get up and dress and I used to walk with him all the way back to his flat, or his hotel rather, on the Left Bank, which was about three miles, I suppose, and would walk all the way back after that.

I haven't seen him since he got married. We didn't part on bad terms, there was no row or anything like that, I was just bitterly disappointed. Anyhow, he left Paris and his home was down elsewhere in the country, and we sort of had a desultory correspondence for a year or two and then that was the end of that.

In the Diplomatic Service one really had to be astonishingly careful. The great centre of gay life in Paris, this was in 1933, was the clubs on the Left Bank in Montmartre and Montparnasse, which I didn't dare to go near. There were also some Smith's Tea Rooms. They were on the Rue de Rivoli, which was rather like a Lyons Corner House in London. You had to get there by two in the afternoon if you wanted to get a table. It was all there among all the public school shields and so on, but I didn't dare to go there either. I mean, as a senior British diplomat one occupied a pretty prominent position. I think that would be true even today, one would be rather careful in that sort of position, which was incidentally one reason why later on I took steps to get myself out of the Foreign Service. Because it was quite plain that one would be uncomfortable. So, later on in 1937, when I was offered the chance of a transfer to the Home Civil Service, I took it very willingly.

There was one friend of mine in the Foreign Office, not anybody I had ever had an affair with, whom in fact I didn't learn for years was gay, because he always trailed a great collection of photographs of girls around with him, had them all over his flat and so on. But I subsequently learnt it was a complete blind.

It was becoming fairly clear then that I was homosexual, by dint of reading Havelock Ellis, reading Edward Carpenter, reading Plato in particular. I had made strenuous efforts to cultivate women but really without any success. That just didn't seem to register in any particular way. I mean it was nice to be with women and all that, but the sort of idea of doing anything was not something that I wanted to do at all.

Havelock Ellis reoriented one into thinking not only that this was possible but it was a thing which actually happened to a number of people and that it was quite natural for me. Not for other people necessarily.

I remember going to buy Havelock Ellis, I don't remember where, whether it was in London or in Paris, but being very much struck. And of course by Plato. I think perhaps then one was reading fairly widely. It was authors like Walter Pater and Winckelmann and people like that, and they all sort of pointed in that direction. They were things that were congenial to read.

In 1934 I came back to England. I became involved in the gay scene in London fairly directly then. One knew one's way about rather by then and, I mean, I'm not sure that the gay scene in London has altered all that much really. I mean there were the pubs and there were clubs. One was perhaps a little more discreet than one needs to be nowadays, and I distinctly remember it was always a very bad sign for people if they wore camel hair coats and suede shoes! I remember when I bought myself a camel hair and suede shoes, I thought I really was coming out. One was casting in one's lot very definitely with the gay community. Of course, a lot of the people in the Foreign Office were gay too. In fact, it was the era, of course, of Burgess and Maclean.

One particularly popular pub in Shepherd Market used to be called the Running Horse, it's now called something else. That was just round the corner from my own club in Piccadilly. So very often after dinner, working in the Foreign Office, I used to go to my club for dinner, then walk round the corner to the Running Horse. In fact, I met several of the waiters from the club there who were off duty. They used to tease one a bit.

The other sort of centres were at the other end of Piccadilly and there was a sort of continual stream up and down Piccadilly from the Running Horse to the clubs and things at the Piccadilly Circus end, which was partly people like me and partly rent and so on. One gradually learnt to distinguish the rent from the rest.

There was a good deal of rent then. I should have thought there probably was more than now because one has to remember that in those days young people were extraordinarily low paid. I mean some members of the forces and so on were all out for something, looking for money.

Before the war, and in fact for some time during the war, one of the great places was the Coventry Street Corner House. That was rather like Smith's Tea Rooms in Paris, you had to be there by about two on Saturday afternoon if you wanted a table for tea. It was tremendously sought after. One went and had tea and spun it out for a number of hours. They used to have very good pianists there, classical pianists who played Chopin rather well. It was not really a picking up place I don't think, it was really somewhere where you went when you had picked up. Then there were the Lyons Brasseries, which were in the basements of the Corner House, also socialising places.

I had a flat in Chelsea at that time, and on the underground from Sloane Square to St James's Park for the Foreign Office, I from time to time saw a marvellously handsome young man, absolutely super. I wondered who he was and so on. I had previously been introduced to Morgan Forster and Joe Ackerley and one or two others in that circle. And one day I went to have dinner at Chez Victor in Wardour Street, which still exists as a matter of fact, and there was Morgan Forster having dinner with this marvellously handsome young man whom I'd seen in the underground. So he introduced us. And after that the handsome young man and I went home together, and that was the start of some very happy occasions.

We lived in my cottage, which my father bought for us. We lived there till the war and then he went into the Friends' Ambulance Unit, as I did. But he joined at an earlier stage and went out to the Middle East and was killed in the desert.

I knew Morgan Forster very well. He was an old friend of mine. I used to see him about once a week when I worked in

Cambridge. He used to come to me and spend the evening listening to gramophone records and so on. And I used to go and see him.

But the people I knew much better were earlier contemporaries of Forster's like Joe Ackerley. I always longed to have an affair with Joe Ackerley, never did, I thought he was desperately handsome. But he obviously wasn't interested in me. His thing was guardsmen or policemen.

One of the things about the war, when it broke out, was that all one's gay friends suddenly appeared in the most gorgeous uniforms, and all joined rather exotic regiments. You've probably heard there was some anti-aircraft defence unit, I think it was somewhere down in Kent, which was wholly gay.

I think it was some MP who organised it, one of the gay MPs, I'm not sure who it was. It became notorious on the gay scene, rather. I was in the Friends' Ambulance Unit, during the war, because of my pacifist convictions. I did not link my homosexuality to liberal political convictions. I saw them as quite separate, I think. Because I don't think I had very liberal political convictions, actually. They were quite separate. Surprisingly enough, the Friends' Ambulance Unit was not at all a homosexual outfit. The number I thought were gay was perhaps rather small in comparison with the outside world.

I think I felt, as I still do, that to go round shooting and gunning people was quite wrong, and still worse if they're handsome young men. One had so many friends of other nationalities. I mean, I corresponded throughout the war and still correspond with a German whom I met in a bar in Paris before the war and who was a prisoner of war. He's now a respectable banker in Frankfurt.

I think the war led to a sort of breaking down of old inhibitions and customs and family ties. A lot of people had affairs with service people, though not necessarily within the services where it was much too dangerous. One now met people and arranged to see them on leave and that sort of thing. The blackout helped undoubtedly.

I think some homosexuals incline towards the feminine, or rather seek a butch partner. I shouldn't have thought that had changed to any great extent. I should have thought, as regards guardsmen and so on, a lot of homosexual people do rather pine after tough young men. Morgan Forster, for example, says somewhere that he longs to be loved by a young man of the working classes; well that's a thing I can understand absolutely.

I think Forster remarks somewhere that working-class people have never had the same sort of hang-ups about homosexuals that the middle-class people have had. They did seem sort of, quite ready to oblige. I don't think they were all homosexual. I think they just obliged and probably quite enjoyed it, and probably made a bit of money out of it. Middle-class people probably tend to think about it a lot more, and have hang-ups about it. Whereas I think working-class people tend to take life as it comes.

I don't know really if attitudes have changed, because, you see, when you get to my age one's friends tend to be married [gay] couples. I mean Bob and I, we've lived together for more than twenty years now. We entertain other couples who have lived together for a great length of time and one doesn't really circulate in the contemporary scene to any great extent. And indeed one hasn't really got much to offer them.

Of course, in the absence of *Gay News,* the advertisement columns of the *New Statesman* were places that one looked at, rather carefully coded advertisements, bachelor seeks another to share house, that sort of thing, I mean, really rather like the *Gay News* advertisements today, but more discreet.

There used to be drag parties which were often very grand, because these people usually had enormous flats and lots of money and it was champagne and that sort of thing. The other thing of course, a great mecca for the gay world, was Lady Malcolm's servants' ball at the Albert Hall every year. She was some very benevolent lady who believed in doing something for the servants, and so every year, at the Albert Hall, she organised this enormous servants' ball. Which I suppose several thousand people used to go to dressed up, and that became a mecca for homosexuals who used to go in all sorts of extraordinary garbs. I went once or twice I think, and I saw young men dressed in a tiger skin or all sorts.

I was dressed rather respectably, as a matter of fact. I went in an Arab costume which I'd been given during the war, with flowing things and a cord round one's head. Lady Malcolm was horrified by it and eventually the thing was brought to an end. The other event, of course, was the Chelsea Arts Ball which was a mixed affair, but again sort of largely patronised by the gay fraternity.

Another great meeting-place was the gallery in Sadler's Wells. There was the ballet, of course, but one used to go up there and one got in for a shilling and stand at the back. That was really quite some pick-up point.

I saw a fair amount of the gay life in Cambridge, because it revolved round one or two particular people who gave parties, and encouraged people to let their hair down. One has the impression, and there again one may be wrong, but has the impression that there aren't nearly the number of parties now that there used to be in those days.

I mean getting an invitation to a party was a great occasion, it was quite easy to get off with somebody handsome, have a marvellous time. More often than not one didn't. And came home feeling rather frustrated. Anyhow there was the possibility.

I think once you've sort of married, as it were, and settled down, you fall out of the network rapidly. After all, people go to parties to get off with people, not meet old married couples like Bob and me!

I lived alone for a time after the relationship with the boy I met through Morgan Forster broke up. Then I met Bob and we've lived together ever since.

Bob and I met towards the end of the war, 1946 or thereabouts, because he'd just been doing his National Service. Then he went into hospital work. And was never free at weekends. So we only met rather occasionally as a matter of fact, and he used to come down to Cambridge for the day sometimes, used to have lunch at college and so on, before going back to the cottage for the weekend.

We lived apart for about ten years initially. He had a flat in London and I had the house in the country. We sort of divided our time. Eventually we found that that was rather unsatisfactory and so we eventually decided that it would be simpler to live in one place all the time.

I found I never had any sort of trouble about my relationship with Bob from my family or friends. There again I think people probably accept situations provided nobody rams it down their throats. So I lived openly with these people, and they were accepted by my parents and I by their parents and so on. But the subject wasn't discussed. An old Cambridge friend of mine said, surely you've discussed it with your parents? Bob had the same suggestion made to him. But our reply was that it would probably have caused a great deal of pain and embarrassment where it would serve no useful purpose. So my parents never knew formally. It was so little a problem that we always had a double room when we stayed at my parents. And the same from my civil servant colleagues, for dinner parties and so on. I think people know that we don't accept invitations separately.

At points in my career which mattered I was careful to tell my establishment officer at the Civil Service the situation. Oh yes. Because it was the case, and I think still is the case, that on the whole homosexuals are not promoted above the rank of assistant secretary in the Civil Service. An old friend of mine, a Scotsman, became involved in a case which had a certain amount of publicity. He had just been promoted to be Under Secretary and he was demoted again. Yes, so when it began to look as though I might be promoted to Under Secretary I certainly didn't want to be there under false pretences, and so I made a point of seeing my establishment officer at that time and making the situation entirely clear to him. I didn't go beyond assistant secretary. I retired some six years ago.

There were a certain amount of problems within the office which could arise. I remember when I was in the Foreign Office, for example, there was an excessively handsome young clerical officer I used to have occasion to come and see and so on, and I should dearly have loved to have seen more of him, but it wouldn't have been at all wise. So I had to keep him at a distance, a long distance.

I was, I think, aware of changing opinions, in the wake of the

Kinsey Report, for instance, or *Wolfenden* proposals. But, there again, I wonder if things have changed as much as people make out. I shouldn't have thought the change in the law affected people's lives much. I think what it has obviously done is to reduce the occasions for blackmail, which is all to the good.

I go back to Cambridge to dine from time to time. I think it has changed in the sense, of course, that the colleges have become co-educational. I think that probably takes the pressure off. I mean before colleges reminded one of rather a relaxed public school. People sort of romped around and so on, but I think the co-education has rather taken the heat off that sort of activity.

What one would like to see, of course, is everybody making less fuss about sexuality altogether. I mean it's preposterous the extent to which it occupies the media. I mean the sort of change I should like to see is one in which nobody really bothers about it, but they are what they are and do what they want to do and that's that, and doesn't cause comment or headlines or anything.

I think one has the impression that the influence of the media is much greater than it was, and also of course that they're much more outspoken than they were. Matters are discussed that would never have been discussed in those days. The curiosity and so on seems to be a bit regrettable, the sort of headlines that one sees.

I don't see much change in the immediate future because I think change takes a very long time. Obviously the present generation is a great deal more relaxed than we were. But no doubt another generation, the next one, will be more relaxed still and less fussed and hung up about it all. But I think it takes a very long time for public attitudes to alter.

I personally think it is ludicrous to have this age of consent business. I mean I don't sort of advocate sex with minors and so on, but if both parties want it, it doesn't do the slightest harm, it probably does them a lot of good. Looking back to my own life, I owe a great deal to a schoolmaster with whom I had an affair. He was an extremely nice man, and I felt I gained nothing but good from it. I think I gained much more than he did out of it because I can't have been very good.

I would like to see the law recognise gay marriages, but I'm not sure how much point it would serve. I mean heterosexual marriage is obviously important from the point of view of the family and the children and all that sort of thing. Whether it's equally important to homosexual partners, I don't really know. Bob and I have always regarded our relationship as akin to a marriage absolutely.

12 A kept life

Bernard was born in Aberdeen, Scotland in 1913, into a large working-class family. He began meeting local gay men from the age of fifteen. He later ran away to London with another boy, wandered the streets and eventually got picked up by an older American. This was the first of a number of relationships with older, wealthy men, including several other Americans. During the 1930s he was essentially a 'kept boy', eventually living with an American lover. After the war they split up. Subsequently, as Bernard says, he became suburban. At the time of the interview he was living alone in a South London terraced house, where the interview took place.

No one seduced me, I think, rather I seduced other people in those days. When I was a very little boy, whenever I met anyone I liked my instinctive thing was to say hello, just a natural thing with me really.

My first real experience was coming home from evening classes. I met this man who was much older than me. I wasn't even sixteen. He was very ugly, I remember, very ugly, with glasses. I didn't want him at all. But there was one night coming home he followed me, and I knew what he wanted. It wasn't that I was afraid of him, I wasn't a bit afraid. But he was so ugly I didn't want to bother with him. The next night, coming home from evening classes, he was there again, at the end of the street waiting for me. Again he followed me.

After a couple of nights I spoke to him, and I found him very funny. He wasn't effeminate, nothing like that, you know, but he started talking about his friends. And in those days (I don't know whether they did this anywhere else) but in that particular spot they used to give each other names, like 'Bebe Daniels'. As far as I knew there was only one Bebe Daniels, that was the film actress. I really thought he meant it. And he said one day he'd take me to meet her! I thought this was wonderful. It never occurred to me to wonder what Bebe Daniels was doing in the North of Scotland, in December! I was excessively naïve!

He turned out to be an enormous man, who twittered! About as wide as this. And he was obviously male and very funny. I loved it. I really did. And I used to go to Bebe Daniels's house every Sunday for months. I didn't say anything, I'd just sit there and listen. It really was wonderful. They all spoke in the local dialect. In retrospect they were very intelligent and, given a chance now, I think that they might have made something of their lives. But obviously they couldn't, there was nothing they could do. With the place being what it was and the people being what they were, those who showed the slightest idea that they were queer, the slightest impression of being gay and they were out anyway. Completely out.

They were all on the dole, there weren't any jobs. And with the additional burden they had it was absolutely hopeless. Absolutely hopeless for them. On Saturday night there was a pub they used to go to that didn't do any business. So if it hadn't have been for them the pub wouldn't have had any business.

I left school when I was fourteen and I used to work hauling enormous baskets of meat in a barrow as a butcher's boy. God, when I think of it,. God knows what they weighed. I had to put the meat down into a ship's hold. It was ghastly, ghastly, and it was really hard. Ten bob a week I got for that.

My father drank mostly. He was a nice man, well of course, there weren't any jobs, but I don't suppose he wanted a job. My family weren't rich. No, good heavens no. Good heavens, anything but. Anything but. I was one of a large family. Most of whom died. I now have a brother and three sisters. But there were vast numbers of them. I remember a little girl. She died at the age of about two, for no apparent reason, as far as I can remember.

Around this time I met a boy called Billy, at Bebe Daniels's house. He was very beautiful. He really was very beautiful, although I didn't fall in love with him. He didn't attend the group at this particular time, because his people were very Presbyterian and hauled him off to church on Sundays. He couldn't do anything about it. But apparently he'd been about since he was thirteen. He didn't work, having left school at the age of fourteen.

I can remember one day he said that he wanted to go to London and I said to him, well why don't you? And he said, I haven't any money. Well, I said, I have, and we arranged to go by ship. All of this group came to see us off. It cost us thirty shillings. Wasn't worth it. It was a ghastly boat. Hugged the coast all the way down. I was violently sick.

When we got to London, the vastly more experienced Billy just sort of disappeared—I can't remember what happened. We'd only been there for a few days. We knew no one and had nowhere to sleep. I didn't even know enough to go look for a room.

I remember walking down Kensington High Street and I was so tired. My feet were so sore and I felt that I could walk if I could get off the pavement and walk in the middle of the street, on the tarmacadam. I was still only sixteen, small. Must have been rather sweet-looking when I think of it!

One night, walking, of all places, along St James's St, this American fellow spoke to me. He just spoke to me, and told me to go and get a room and meet him tomorrow. He must have been a very nice man. Which I did. I took him to the room. He was a man about forty-nine, and his name was Carl. And then, that day, we went to the zoo. I knew him two days, I think. And then he said goodbye, he was going back to America. My rent was paid for a couple of weeks, or something. And then came a cablegram from this man, mid-ocean. Apparently he had been thinking. He had decided to send me some money every month, on the condition that I went to school. And as a result of that, I went home to Scotland. I went to a secretarial school, and did this for about nine months.

In the meantime, you see, all these Bebe Daniels people, they all got to know about this, and they thought this was marvellous, wonderful. Because I wasn't a bit clever, wasn't a bit clever. It just happened. I was still only seventeen.

The American came, after about six months, he came back to see me in Aberdeen. I took him home. My mother liked him very much. He really was a very nice man and she didn't know what was happening, there was positively no danger at all, because, poor old soul, she didn't know there was such a thing.

Shortly afterwards I returned to London and I really started looking for a job. But I hadn't had any experience and I couldn't really do anything except type a bit and I started to do shorthand. My spelling always had been quite good so I felt quite confident about that. However poor Carl, he could scarcely have unpacked back in Illinois when I met a very handsome American, a very handsome one indeed, who had a return ticket. He'd come over here for a holiday. He'd originally been a New Zealander. His family was still in New Zealand and he said to me, look, why don't you come to the States? I've got my first-class ticket. If I cash it in we could both go third class to New York. There's a car in New York and I want to change it for a new one when we get there. We can go from there to San Francisco. He was twenty-nine.

I decided to go. On our way to San Francisco we called at Carl's home, in a small town just west of Chicago. We stayed at a tourist camp in a cabin, and I rang Carl, who was absolutely astonished. I think he must have been a little bit apprehensive too. However, he said, well, come over. So I went.

Carl looked after his ageing mother, his sisters and an Englishman. I shouldn't really say this, but I don't think I was the first Briton that Carl had collected. I think that this Englishman had originally been Carl's property, who, very naughtily, had married his sister. Awful. I remember, as a matter of fact, that Carl had very angrily told me about the marriage. It was not that he minded losing him, but the thought that he'd married his sister made him very angry. He was completely queer this English fellow, completely queer. Immediately he saw me he started making camp remarks, which I ignored.

We stayed for three days. And then we went back to the tourist camp and continued our journey, with Carl's blessing. I kept in touch with him for several years. Then I didn't, I stopped.

My friend and I went on to San Francisco. And then, you know, the traditional American money-making. All the conversation's money, how to make money. How he'd made some money. How he intended making more money. It bored me. Bored me to tears, I mean I couldn't care less about that subject. As long as I had enough to eat and a place to sleep, that was all I wanted.

Well now, liquor had just come out of prohibition or something. He said, I want to start a liquor store, so come and work for me. And he took a shop, do you know San Francisco, do you? Took a shop in San Francisco, on Powell Street which is just off Market Street, which is one of the better streets in San Francisco. And installed me. I didn't like it. Didn't like it a bit. So I only stuck that for nine months.

In the meantime, while I was sinking in this shop, he was out discovering about his queerness. And he met a fellow called Del, Delmar I expect it was. Delmar. And Delmar used to come to the shop to pick him up. I didn't object to Delmar. I didn't object to whatever he did, I couldn't care less. No, not a bit jealous. Not a bit. But I was lonely and I resented being lonely.

This was during the depression, remember, I was still only seventeen or so in any case. I stayed in San Francisco for nine months. And then I said I'm going. I want to get back, wanted to get back to good old London. So I got back to London.

There were places people used to go to in those days, for example the Criterion, in Piccadilly Circus where there was a bar and tables. Enormous place downstairs, you could sit there all night with a beer. There was a circle bar at the Palladium, I remember the barmaid, her name was Julie or something. You could get a Rover ticket at the Palladium. People used to stand along the back of the circle and there about. By this time I knew all about prostitution. People told me about it. They used to go to certain places every night to Piccadilly, the Palladium. For some reason, a lot of these people who were on the game, on their nights off when they couldn't be bothered anymore, used to go to the Palladium.

Sex as such never did mean a lot to me. The queerness, you

understand, did. I never have been interested in sex, that sort of way. It never occurred to me to go out looking for people. In any case, even in those days it wasn't as wild as it is now. People had to be more careful in those days. Used to meet people, but I mean to talk to them was enough for me. I didn't really talk to them, rather listen to them.

I was now about eighteen. One night at the Palladium I met a queer fellow whom I knew, and with him he had this man, quite an elderly man. Well obviously he was so old, to me at the age of eighteen, that I couldn't possibly be interested. And the fellow he was with gave him my address. He came to see me the very next day. He was an Englishman. He's the only one I feel guilty about. He lived in Devon, was married and had two boys. He'd been in the Indian Army. He said, well what do you want to do? Well to be honest I didn't really want to do anything. So he said, would you like to go on the stage? So I said, yes, it'd like to go on the stage, but I can't do anything. Well, he said, I'm going to teach you.

He gave me enough money to live on, and my fees. For about two years I didn't go! To this day I don't know where the Royal Academy of Dramatic Art is! I felt very bad about that. I feel very bad about that now, although I didn't at the time. I also visited him. He had a beautiful house. He had no shame about me. He took me down to his house in Taunton and introduced me to his wife as a friend. His naivety must have been extreme. He was about fifty, fifty-five perhaps.

In the end I met another American. Not only was he very rich but he was very generous. This great American was thirty-eight. Young, virile, loved the theatre, loved going to restaurants. Which I loved too. Whereas this Taunton fellow he'd just look at me for days, he didn't really want sex, he wanted to cuddle me, you know. Just get into bed and cuddle me all night long. Thoroughly nice man. Anyway, this American came on the scene. For about three weeks, during which this old man was back in Taunton, I was being taken to the Savoy Hotel and to a restaurant in Chelsea called The Queens. This American lived in Pall Mall. I thought this was wonderful. He said, go and take a house. So I said, all right. I took this studio in Chelsea.

When the Taunton fellow came back to London I confessed to him that I was leaving him. He wept and he said, you've let me down. Of course I didn't believe him. I didn't want to. And that was that.

I met the man from Taunton by accident a while later, looked up and there on the balcony was this fellow. He rushed down, let me in, and he had had the most terrible tragedy. He and his wife had a very big house just outside Taunton. And behind the house was a hill, with a sort of aqueduct. The weather had been very hot, and somewhere along the line some bushes near this aqueduct had caught fire. Apparently they felt it might damage the water supply, so his wife rushed up to mend it and she died. This was only a few weeks after I ditched him. So, the poor man, he was practically a zombie by this time. And that was the last time I saw him. He died quite soon after.

The [new] American was a bastard. He was not exclusively homosexual. He used to mention the telephonist where he worked, she was a married woman. He mentioned her quite often. But I used to keep away from discussing that sort of thing. There wasn't any trouble. I kept out of people's normal lives, those people who had normal lives. He supported me. We had a housekeeper. I didn't look after the house. He used to go off to work, but I went to the races, to the dogs. We were together about seven years.

Then came war, many years later. I volunteered but they said it wouldn't be worth it, just go home and wait. Sure enough, about four months later I was called up. There were tears and I went off to the war at the age of twenty-seven. After my initial training I was posted to Blackpool, to a driver-training regiment, as a permanent member of staff. I loathed it, calling these people, sir, and all that nonsense. If the officer had been queer I wouldn't mind calling him sir, but I did resent it if they weren't queer. Blackpool was also filled with airmen, and there were bars there we used to go into. For the sake of something to do when I was off duty in the evening, we used to gamble. I remember going to the dogs and winning lots of money and taking about twenty of them to an enormous restaurant in Blackpool.

This American used to come and visit me now and again. When America came into the war he went into the war. The only difference it apparently made to him was just that he wore a uniform. He'd joined up as a captain and finally became a colonel.

He never used to write to me while in this country, always telephone calls, you know, and I thought, oh this is the American way. Then I was posted overseas to Europe. I never did any fighting and never any sex, because, as I explained, I never went looking for sex, ever. Before I went into the army sex used to find me. If I wanted it I took it. Still he never wrote to me.

When it was all over, I'd been in the army for six years and I was now thirty-three. When I was demobbed they took me home to Scotland. They had put me ashore with hundreds of others. And I called the American at about three o'clock in the morning. He was astonished, he said, but Bernard this is awful because at six o'clock tomorrow night I go to New York, I go to Washington or something. So I said, all right, it doesn't matter. I felt that something was not quite right. I finally got home and that afternoon I had a telegram (we weren't on the telephone at home). He asked if I would telephone him before he left. But there was something not quite right. What had actually happened, he'd been in bed with somebody at his room. When I got through on the telephone, the telephonist said I'm afraid he's gone.

After three months I came back to London. I'd heard nothing, nothing at all. I took a room in Ebury Street. I got a job. The first job I'd ever had in my life. With people who made and sold pumps. I really was quite good at it.

Incidentally, most of my army leaves during the war were ruined, because he lost my [civilian] clothes. It sounds silly to say it, but all of my suits were made in Savile Row, on his account. He said he got on to the train, coming down from Blackpool or something, and the porter took this bag containing my clothes, and put them in the luggage van. I don't believe it. And when he got there, he forgot about them. Forgot to go down and collect them. And he said, when he finally remembered, they'd gone.

Now, of course, you couldn't possibly buy a suit these days. No matter how much money was available, you just couldn't buy clothes. And I screamed and wept and I remember the waiters coming and looking at me in astonishment in the tea rooms. He said, it doesn't matter, I'll get you some clothes. He tried, he really tried. Couldn't. So there I was wearing my dirty old bloody uniform still.

I must have written to him, because a call came and said, would I come to Paris for a couple of days. So we met in Paris and stayed at the Georges Cinq. The second night we went to a bar, it was crowded as always. And he said, you wait there, I'll go and get a drink. And he went, pushed his way through the crowd to get a drink. And I waited. And I waited. And I waited. For twenty minutes, half-an-hour. I could see him at the bar. Having a drink with somebody he met at the bar. So I thought, oh to hell with this, I'm going. As I left the bar, he came running after me. Bernard, Bernard, he's calling me, Bernard, Bernard, what's the matter, Bernard? I didn't turn. I got back to the hotel and went to bed. There was the bottle of scotch. And I put it to my mouth, glug, glug, glug, and down it went. After about ten minutes he came with a beautiful young boy. When he came in he said he wanted to give the boy a drink. I said, I drank it. So he rang for more scotch. I was so angry I leapt from the bed stark naked and beat him up. The boy fled. I probably would have killed him, if he'd been left alone, but he was screaming for help. They beat the door down, the waiters, and I was carried out by the police screaming like a maniac all the way downstairs.

The police said I would have to go back to London. So I said, but how? I haven't got a ticket, unless you give me my money (which was at the hotel). I said, you'll see that the traveller's cheques are made out in my name, if you care to send for them. So they produced this book of cheques and the policemen obviously knew the entire story, that I was kept. I was so ashamed. That was it, finish. That was the end. I never saw him again.

That was the end of, of that sort of thing completely, completely, and I became suburban. For the rest of my life I had a job. I went to an office in Waterloo.

At this time any sex was casual and seldom. Very, very

seldom. As I say, you see, I wasn't terribly interested in sex. Round about the Taunton time there was a woman involved. A ferocious woman. I think she thought she seduced me, little did she know! I used to sleep with her, quite successfully apparently, according to her. I used to sleep with her, but I had to get out of that, very dreary. She was possessive. I quite liked sleeping with her. On occasions I found it a bit of a bore. It lasted until the American came on the scene.

But since the American I've just had one night stands. Mostly unenthusiastic. I was never a primary mover. I never went cottaging. I met them in streets. I think gay people today are very lucky. Insomuch as if they don't want to, they have to conceal nothing. Homosexuality wasn't on the TV, or even the radio, never. It was never, never, never mentioned. It was just ignored, it just didn't exist.

I was a prodigious reader, but I didn't read anything on the subject of homosexuality, it never occurred to me. I just took it for granted, as something completely natural. I did wish that I could have been open about it, but one couldn't. None of my family have ever known. So far as I know. It's never been discussed. It's too late now because I couldn't do it without being embarrassed about it, no matter how willing they were and I was, I wouldn't do it. I wouldn't talk on the subject.

In the 1930s I think that people who didn't discover the subject until they were in their twenties and whose extreme youth was gone, I think they must have been very unhappy. When I discovered the subject, I wasn't even a youth, I was just a boy. I was, say, about fifteen when Bebe Daniels came along. That still makes me laugh, that whole business of giving girl's names. I didn't approve of it. I don't approve of it.

My likes have never varied, I've never liked boys. Even when I was a boy I never liked boys to go to bed with. I've never liked old men either. People I've wanted have always been sort of mature, thirty, forty.

13 An exile's life

Barry was born in Wantage, Berkshire in 1913, into a middle-class family. His father was a headmaster. After Oxford University, Barry went to France for a year, then began teaching in England. Subsequently he joined the British Council, partly, as he says, to escape the intolerance of England. As a teacher of English for the Council he lived successively in Greece, Cyprus, Egypt, India and the Congo. At the time of the interview he had retired, but was a prominent member of a local gay group. He was interviewed in his home by the River Thames in West London.

I was born on 1 June 1913, at Wantage in Berkshire. It was then in Berkshire. My father was a headmaster at a school in Wantage.

When I was six, we moved to Rotherham, in South Yorkshire, where my father was headmaster of the grammar school. I myself started school in the junior department of the grammar school. But then, in 1924, he got the headship of a Brighton school and we went down there and I did, in fact, go right through that school.

I've always rather wondered about the moment I realised I was homosexual, honestly. I obviously enjoyed playing about with other boys at school, but then so did a lot of others. I always preferred slightly younger ones. It was just before I was sixteen. And then a young master at that school gave me quite a long talk, shall we say, I won't say he made a pass, not right at the beginning. He was the first person to use the word homosexual in my hearing, it was the first time I'd ever heard it. And that perhaps put an idea into my head, I don't know. I knew that sort of thing wasn't very well looked on by people in authority, of course. It was considered dirty. In the Church of England, rather definitely so. Both my grandfathers were Methodist ministers but my father had been confirmed into the Church of England when he went to Oxford. My mother was confirmed into the Church of England when she married. I always had, indeed still have, a tremendous respect for the Church of England and, in fact, of Christianity. I do go to church, not a lot, perhaps I should go more. I go three times a year, to communion and the feasts and so on.

I had religious qualms about my sexuality, and then I decided it was really rather too much fun to give up. And so went on with it. I must say, it wasn't a conscious decision. Not really. At the age of puberty when one begins to develop sexually, it affects one's emotions particularly, and first of all, at that time, my emotions were directed to religion. And then gradually moved over to sex. Put it that way.

I don't think I've ever used the word homosexuality and I don't think I've ever told anybody I was, really ever, until quite recently. But then it's more or less taken for granted and, after all, it's a very different situation now.

It wasn't until my early or mid-twenties that I first heard the word 'queer'. Which is a word I still use with my contemporaries. With no sneer or other sort of deteriorative implication at all. I first heard the word queer from somebody I picked up on the seafront at Worthing. I dislike the word gay very strongly. The main reason is because it deprives me of a perfectly good English word in its proper sense. It seems to me to be a very bad choice. Second, it's a sign of the American influence on our language and, as you probably gathered, I know a certain amount about the English language. Well, it's part of my life really.

When I went to Oxford, I had a certain amount of experience. At that time I had a tendency to fall in love with people who were not homosexual. And it was a hopeless sort of situation, and rather miserable, as you can imagine. At Oxford there were at least two with whom I never had any sexual experience at all because they just were not interested. They knew how I felt. At any rate, one of them certainly did, and gave me a long talking to. He said, look, this is no good. (I could give you his name but I won't. That I won't do. I mean, he's still alive as far as I know and I followed his career more or less. It's a public career.)

I always hated ball games. Particularly cricket. Football as well. On my father's advice, may I say, I took up rowing, and was very much in the rowing set in the college. Any real sex that one had was falling into bed with somebody after a boat club dinner when one was a bit tipsy. On only one occasion there was something said. The particular person said, good thing you left when you did last night, because the Dean came in looking for people who had climbed into college over the wall. I went pale with terror when he told me. I often think it's a good thing that I didn't find other homosexual meeting-places.

After I came down from Oxford, I had a year in France, and it wasn't until after I got back from France that this particular master who had used the word homosexual to me at the age of fifteen became, in fact, probably my greatest friend. He was older than I was and I never wanted to go to bed with anybody older than myself, ever. Though I did do it once or twice.

He started talking about cottages in Brighton. That has been something in my life that I tried to resist, because of its danger. I never encountered either the law or queer-bashers in cottages, I'm very glad to say. I had my pocket picked once or twice. I was aware of the legal dangers, very much so. To the extent of buying the *News of the World* every Sunday, to keep abreast with the court cases. Unless they were very bad cases, most of the papers would not report them. I remember very vividly the Montagu case, in the early 1950s and John Gielgud in the early 1950s but that was much later in my life and, at that later period, I was living with a young man here in London, for a short time anyway.

When I came back from France, I got a job teaching French and German in a secondary school in Hove. Cottaging went on to a certain extent at the same time, but there were times when I was terrified. I remember teaching French to a class and looking out of the window where I saw an errand boy on his bicycle whom I'd met at the cottage the night before. It terrified me. Unnecessarily I'm quite sure, because if he'd seen me he would have been as frightened as I was.

A friend of mine lent me Havelock Ellis. With strict instructions to hide it from everybody. I think it was *Sexual Inversion*, but I forget what it was called. This man was somebody who had been at the same school, who was older than I am now. He was a solicitor and he took a certain amount of interest in me, in fact. As I say, he was older than I was, I think he hoped for an affair with me, at that time in the thirties. He used to take me up to London to theatres and that sort of thing. Which was very nice. He lent me Havelock Ellis, as I say, with strict instructions to hide it from everybody because in fact it was illegal at that time I believe, or so he said. It reinforced what I'd been thinking for a long time. I found it interesting, of course.

Why a particular person is homosexual is a very difficult question. I wish it could be answered. If it could be generally proved, or at any rate generally explained by psychiatrists, doctors, what you will, then the general public would get the opinion that homosexuality is born rather than caused by seduction. It would make a very great deal of difference to our situation.

I knew I wanted sex, as we all do. I did not go for much younger people, but the fact that anybody was older was, to use a modern expression, a turn-off really. Almost literally that, I mean, if one discovered that a certain person was even a year or two older, it was enough to turn me off completely, I think. I was interested in men aged from puberty onwards, up to about thirty-five.

There was a pub in Hove at that time, in the thirties, the Star of Brunswick. It was a little pub, behind the Dudley Hotel. It was notorious. It centred round Terence Rattigan. I was far too frightened to go there, to be honest, except once, with this schoolmaster friend of mine. We thought we'd have a look in and see what it was like. It so frightened me that I never went again. We didn't like the idea of getting to be known by people like that. It was the only gay pub I knew of in England. I wouldn't have minded meeting them on the seafront after, but not in that sort of rather blatant way.

I would have liked a relationship very much. Very much. And that's why I went abroad. I got this job with the British Council to teach English abroad. I thought there would be more opportunities, that I would be freer. My first posting was in Greece. As it turned out it was Salonika, not Athens, and it was even more restricted than it had been in this country. But that was only the beginning because then I went to Athens and met quite a lot of people. And the whole thing became clearer. It became clearer what I should do in Greece to meet people.

The Greeks tended not to consider themselves homosexual. Except for a very small group, whom one tended to avoid because they were too obvious. When I first went to Salonika a colleague and I lodged together. He had a fiancée here in London, but quite soon after we got there, he began to take up with a Greek girl, and eventually they married. She was very broad-minded and I got to know them quite well. There was never any secret of my homosexuality with the three of us. It was a very nice, happy relationship. I saw them a lot in various parts of the world and here, in London. I remember on one occasion, in Cyprus, they came on a visit and she asked me, don't you ever regret being queer? My answer was, if I were not I would be a different person, I mean I would accept whatever it was. I think that has always been my attitude, really. It has been a very deep part of my life.

At that time I did not form any relationships. You see, that was 1938–9. Greece, of which I'm still extremely fond, has always had a reputation for homosexuality, since classical times. In the thirties there were western Europeans living in that part of the world simply because sex, on the whole, was easy if you knew how to do it. It still is. Before the war, homosexuality in Greece was so prevalent, side-by-side with heterosexuality, that there never were any bars or pubs or anywhere to pick anybody up, and certainly not cottages. That all came into Greece with the war.

I was there until 1941, when, in front of the Germans, we escaped to Egypt. There it was terrific. A lot more impersonal, well that's not the word, a lot more 'anonymous', shall we say. But there was a constant fear of getting to be known among my employers, the British Council, as a member of the homosexual set.

One forestalled any requests for money [for pick ups] by dishing out fairly soon in Greece and Egypt. A lot of it was very mercenary. In the UK I had my pocket picked once or twice, but I don't think I was ever asked blatantly for money. Apart from anything else, I wasn't all that well off, although from the middle class. In a country like Greece or Egypt, one is a European and therefore rich. Which is quite different from here.

As a rule, one wouldn't have gone to bed with one's homosexual friends. Partly because most of them were my age or older. Second, because the natives of the country were far more exciting! I had quite an affair with a Greek boy, but that wasn't until we went back to Greece after the war. I lived with him, or rather he lived with me, in Athens. That was the summer of 1946. I was abroad for six or seven years in that part of the world. I came back in 1945 for the first time. And then regular leaves after that, every two years. I was back in Greece and delighted to be there.

The country was still very badly organised. This was one of the most idyllic moments of my life. I went off to the islands, to the Cyclades, by myself. I think it was July or August, and I got into a relationship with a young Greek who, as I say, lived with me in Athens, when we went back. We spent a few weeks in boats, bathing. It was absolutely idyllic, I look back on it as absolutely marvellous. His father had been something quite prominent on the island. Middle-class, indeed. He had collaborated with the Italians, and I suppose the Germans, and was at that time in prison on another island. I still see him on the rare occasions when I go back to Athens. He mixes with the homosexual group in Athens. He's out for tourists, but he never married. I think he was more homosexual than most Greeks are.

I think it was probably in the Middle East during the war that I first started going to Turkish baths. I had a Greek friend who was rather a blatant queen and slightly older than myself, in Salonika. He used to take me to the baths. There were two or three really rather beautiful Turkish baths, steam baths. They were built like Byzantine churches. And we used to go there for an afternoon. Quite a lot goes on in places like that, or did. There were a certain amount in Athens, and there were one or two in Cyprus in the middle of Nicosia, of the same sort. And very pleasant they were. They were nice places to go to of an evening when you'd had a little bit to drink and were beginning to feel like it. The young men, they were always young men who massaged you, were all very nice. One got to know them quite well.

There were also Turkish baths in London. There was the Harrow Road Turkish baths. It was situated just off Edgware Road. This was in the forties. It was open six days and six nights a week. It opened at 9 o'clock on Monday morning, and didn't close until 9 o'clock on the following Sunday morning, when it was open to women. I remember, I was there one evening, on leave from somewhere, and somebody said to me, do you often come here? And I said, as often as I can when I'm in London. It was terrific. It really was. Everything went on there, fairly discreetly.

There was one evening, again when I was on leave, when I went there. I was staying with a friend in Maida Vale, and I said, well I'm going to Harrow Road tonight. He said, in that case, I'll ring up a friend of mine and he can come and spend the night with me, so don't come home for the night. Well, I got there, I got undressed and I had a bath and massage and all the rest of it, and was lying on the bed. They had cubicles with two beds, with curtains. And the man in the other bed suddenly started hugging and kissing me and got into bed with me. Immediately Harry, who was the old man in charge of the place, got on the rampage, for some reason. He'd never done so before and I never knew him to after. But he said, here come on, you can't do that. You'd better leave. Well, it was very awkward, and it wasn't my initiative at all, I was furious. I just took no notice. Pushed the man out and went to sleep. And stayed the night.

I think most of the Turkish baths have gone now. There was one in Jermyn Street, the Savoy, and there was the one in Russell Square, which was one of the real old-fashioned ones, got up like a Turkish one. That one, I found to be rather dangerous and mercenary, but Harrow Road was fine. Then there was one down in Bermondsey, attached to a swimming baths. There were always one or two boys on the make, but one got to recognise them. I do not think they were straight, because, after all, a boy's got to be pretty well bisexual if not homosexual, to do those sort of things. You can tell whether a boy is interested or not, can't you? When he's got nothing on.

There were no cottages in Greece until after the war, until the British troops got them going. I went cottaging here whenever I had the opportunity, honestly. It did rather dominate my thoughts and I felt guilty in a good many ways, I suppose. There was the thought that really one shouldn't do that sort of thing, you know. And also the thought that one might be caught doing it. I was pretty careful. I always used stand-up cottages, I would never have gone into a cubicle. Never.

There wasn't a great deal of writing on the walls in those days. It didn't play any part in my thoughts. There used to be long stories written up on cubicle walls though. I remember spending quite a lot of pennies going into those places and seeing if there was anything to read. Yes, I'd forgotten that.

Anywhere in the Near and Middle East, to put it frankly, they always want to fuck you. Once that is dealt with, then perhaps they will be prepared for something else as well. They might even demand that you fuck them. But they have all this Muslim thing. Greece for many centuries was ruled by the Turks, and that Muslim attitude, that sex for men is only penetration, prevails all over that part of the world. Although not, strangely enough, in India where I had five years. There was a clear distinction between the Muslims and the Hindus. I was in India in one of the most important Muslim cities, Hyderabad, and there was quite a lot of picking up went on, although there were no cottages as such. But one could tell immediately by the attitude of the person one was picking up, whether he was Hindu or Muslim. A Hindu was much more ready to reciprocate. Quite apart from the fact that the Muslims are all circumcised and the Hindus are not.

It was not the sort of thing that I wanted to do for a long time. Either way. It struck me as going a bit too far. In this country [Britain] there was, I think, relatively little fucking. I did have a friend in Hove, when I was teaching, whom I picked up not in a cottage but on the seafront, and I used to go and visit him on my afternoon off. He, in fact, was being kept by an older man whom I never met, in a flat in Hove. I used to ring him up and go down there for a good afternoon's sex once a week. That was good and that was really the first time that I ever did anything about anal penetration. And I must say I quite enjoyed it. But I didn't do a great deal, either way, for some years after that.

I can't say I was happy with my homosexuality, but I certainly didn't want to go and tell anybody and ask for help or anything of that sort. The thing that mainly worried me was the fact that my parents wanted me to get married, and that I could not, to use the modern expression, 'come out'. That was out of the question. My mother wouldn't have known what I was talking about. There's no doubt of that at all. And it would have been a cruelty to try and make her understand. And that is something that I am very prepared to put over to any of these young people who censure me for not being so willing as they are to come out.

I think my father knew, after all he was a lifelong schoolmaster. I think he knew and rather rejected it. There was one occasion, when I took a boyfriend home in the early fifties, when I was living with somebody in London. I took him home, rather ill-advisedly, and he wasn't very nice and drank rather more than he should. I remember my father saying, very surprisingly, why can't you get somebody a bit more stable? But that was the only time that anything of that sort passed between us. I was very fond of both of them really, my mother more than my father, of course that's a typical situation isn't it? and would dearly have loved to please her, but I couldn't. I've never been to bed with a woman.

I did consider a marriage of convenience, but decided against it. Several people advised against it and I quite agree. I think that is absolutely awful. Unless it is an out and out lesbian who might be trusted. What I dislike is a woman making a pass and the awful situation that that puts you into. In those days it wasn't enough just to say I'm gay, because you couldn't say that. She wouldn't have understood, and if she did, there's no fury like a woman spurned. I've always been quite open about my homo-sexuality with homosexuals. It would be wrong not to be.

I got VD in Greece and was terrified, of course. It was gonor-rhoea. It was useful knowing Europeans of my age or older in Greece who were versed in this sort of thing. There was a lot more VD in the Middle East than there was here. Mine was 'frontal' gonorrhoea. I was taken first of all to a homosexual doctor. He was not a leading specialist at all, he said, oh yes, that's all right, go to so and so and tell him it's a woman. Which I did. There were great big tablets, and then there were washes every couple of days to have one's cock washed out. It was before penicillin, which only came in with the war and this was 1938. In any case, for some years after the war it was still very difficult for civilians in that part of the world to get hold of penicillin.

Later on, in Greece after the war, one or two of my friends, one about my age, were sent to a gay doctor in Athens. This was about 1947 or 1948. He knew the doctor was gay because he proposed at one point. Quite a lot of people insisted on 'French letters' in those days. I would never use one; which was proba-bly a mistake, but there.

I picked up this young man outside the cottage at South Kensington station during the summer of 1952. I'm quite good on dates because it gives us something to hang things on to. He was an Australian and I was then working in Cyprus again. I was really very fond of him. He was the one my father remarked on. When I got back to Cyprus that autumn, 1952, I was on leave and I brought him out there. We lived there, very riskily, for a bit, and then I applied for a period in London, and got it. And that was the summer of the Coronation, yes, 1953. And so from that summer, for eighteen months, we lived together. That was the period of the Montagu scandal and Gielgud. It wasn't an equal relationship, equal either in age or financially. He began to become dependent on me financially. We had always been drinking a lot and he began to drink a great deal more. It's a long, complicated story. I don't know where he is now but I'm told that he's gone back to Australia. I rather hope he has. There could never have been the sort of intimate intellectual relation-ship that one depends on when one gets to this sort of age.

The British Council were surprisingly lenient about homo-sexuality. A friend of mine, I won't go into any more detail than this, working in a large European city, got into trouble with the local police, and was given twenty-four hours to leave the country. It was announced in the office bulletin that he had been transferred to a job in the London office. We had an expression, so and so has been grounded, which meant that they wouldn't send you abroad again, you see. But provided you could hold a job in the London office, and indeed why not, they were perfectly prepared to keep you on, probably because they didn't want the scandal of sacking anybody.

My three big affairs have been first with that boy in Greece, he was twenty-one when I met him. Then, with this Australian mainly here, and then with an Indian who was married and had children, which I found quite exciting! He was a pick-up in a public garden. One hot night. There he was standing there, having a pee in the dark and the pin lights, making quite sure that I could see his cock. It was as blatant as that. That relation-ship was complicated. He quarrelled with his wife and sent her back to the village. It was some time before he would admit to me that he was married. He was in an awkward position anyhow. But he said that he'd got a taste for being sucked off by older men. There were no cottages, but it started when he was on the station to catch a train and went to have a pee in a 'cottage' and found his cock in an older man's mouth. That gave him a taste for that, quite apart from the fact that he was otherwise completely 'normal', which is the word I use. He was a very nice companionable person to have.

I lost touch with him, but I've got one or two friends in India on the look out for him. He was in the government audit department, and came from south India, where we met, but he was liable to be sent anywhere in the country, in the old British tradition, at quite short notice. And this whether he'd got accommodation for his family or not. When I left he was already in a different part of south India. I remember then that we kept up a very good correspondence. But, when I was moved from India to what was then the ex-Belgian Congo, Leopoldville, the correspondence became more difficult. I think he was busy and so on. So I've lost him. But I may catch up with him again. I've been back to India working for the British Council, and I had one of these Indian friends of mine staying here last October. I gave him all the particulars, and he said he would keep an eye open.

The Congo was a complete blank sexually. That has convinced me that you can do without sex, what you can't do without happily at all is somebody to talk to. There was nobody, except one rather tiresome queen in the British Embassy, who wouldn't come across at all. One only had to look at him to know. And that meant I had nobody to talk to at all, and no sex at all. I could have gone out into the main street of an evening and picked up a black whore. A black boy. I know that, because they were parading around on the boulevard opposite the big open-air café where all the Europeans went.

I realise now that there was perhaps another man, an Italian. He was a very nice man who worked for UNESCO, who would probably have come across, come out to me. But it was all complicated by the fact that I finished up with a coronary thrombosis and came home very ill. My impression is that the Africans are much less inclined to that sort of thing than anybody I've come across.

The only time I've ever had any real contact with guardsmen was in Cyprus during the war. This was just after the fall of Syria. The French had hold of Syria until some two or three years after de Gaulle took over the French forces outside France. It was eventually decided by the British High Command that we had to do something about Syria and Lebanon, i.e. invade it, and they used the Guards for that. So, during that summer, groups of guardsmen, I can't tell you how many, used to come to Cyprus for a rest, and they were put up at the best hotel in Kyrenia, where I was working. They were delighted to find a European who could talk to them and they were very ready for sex. They liked hospitality, but no more 'payment' than that. They liked a drink and they liked a meal, but nothing more than that. In fact, they used to give parties at the hotel for the British people in the place. And those were lavish.

From Brighton it used to be quite the thing to go and spend

an evening or even a weekend in Portsmouth, with the Navy. And there were pubs there that were patronised by the Navy who were all at any rate sympathetic. The Navy was famously sensible about it. Whether they would go to bed with you or not is another matter. Very often they paid you. One had a very good impression of the Navy from that point of view. They were friendly, pleasant, amusing, ready to talk, some of them were ready for sex. They would give you about, oh, five bob, something of that sort. I remember paying a boy half-a-crown in London and considering that I'd done him rather well. That was both the value of money and the standard.

I knew of what was called the meat rack, that terrace below the National Gallery in Trafalgar Square. I used to be a member of the University Club which was facing out on to the statue of George III in Cockspur Street. And sometimes, having had a little more to drink than necessary, I would walk out late at night, but nothing very much ever happened.

There are organisations now which there never could have been before. You see, it was a great risk to give a party. I remember a case in Brighton, in the thirties. I wasn't there fortunately, but some young queen had been turned down by his boyfriend or something and, in a fit of pique, went out into the street, straight up to a policeman and said, there is immorality going on up there. Are you going to investigate? The whole lot were arrested. I don't think that would happen now, because I don't think the policeman would do anything.

I joined CHE in 1971, just after I retired. I did a certain amount of summer school in Europe for the British Council that summer. When I came back in September I thought, well now I'm settling down here, and I've got to make a life for myself. I was looking down the deaths on the back page of *The Times*, as I always do every day because they're of far more interest to me now than births or marriages, and caught the word homosexuality. It was in fact an advertisement for CHE, which I'd never heard of. I wrote off straight away sending a subscription for thirty shillings, and have been a member of the organisation ever since. I'm very much in favour of CHE as a social thing, I don't mind so much about the campaigning, let them get on with that if they like. But I do think that as a social organisation it is as good as we can get. If only there had been something of that sort in my youth, that's all. My life would have been very different, I've often said that. I think if, in the thirties, there had been any sort of organisation of that sort, I might in fact have struck up an affair and settled down, probably never have gone abroad at all. Going abroad was an attempt to get away from the repression in this country.

I've always been vaguely right, politically, but not too much so. I'm very clear about my political opinions now. And of course, they laugh in CHE, so many of those left-wing boys. They will argue with me for a bit and then they'll realise it's no good going on and we become good friends. I've strong views about British politics and indeed European politics, or even American politics at the moment, but I don't think they're connected with my homosexuality at all really.

I've had one or two awkward experiences with lesbians in these last few years. I believe that even out and out lesbians resent it if a man does not make a pass, or at any rate does not treat them as a female woman. Many of them do, certainly, I won't say all. Some are prepared to be sensible about it. There are one or two women on the committee of the Group. I've been a member of that since the beginning in 1971. There have been women who've come and gone, some of them good friends, up to a point, as far as one can have good friends of that sort. Although it was a great relief, at Nottingham last year [1978] when the women withdrew. In my opinion, they're far more aggressive than we are. And I can do without that aggression. I've no particular principles about it, and when *Gay News* said that men wept when the women withdrew, I thought, what balls, really. Almost all the men there, if you got them quietly aside, they would have agreed that it was a good thing.

The prospects are I suppose eventually for a further change in the law. The age of consent is too high, much too high. I'd like to see it the same as for heterosexuals. The rest I think is a question of educating the population.

I was invited to dinner the other day by a friend of mine who was a member of my club and who I know is bisexual. He is in fact married. I found myself sitting next to a woman of about forty, and she turned to me and she said, your wife isn't here, and I replied, I heard myself say it and I couldn't believe it, I turned and I said, no, I'm homosexual. It rather stunned her! And it put an end to the conversation for the moment. Then we talked about something quite different, quite amicably, may I say. I mean she didn't reject me and that sort of thing.

Now I'm much less promiscuous than I was. I don't make a pass unless I'm pretty sure, not only of being accepted but, at the same time, of feeling that I want to go on with it. I think, in other words, I wouldn't make a pass at anybody unless it was made pretty clear from his side that he wanted it. I hate being rejected. That's a terrible fear.

What little sex I get is through CHE really. I wouldn't ever put my hand on a man's cock in a cottage now, to be absolutely frank. In fact, three or four months ago in a cottage, a young man made it perfectly clear that that is what he wanted, and I was terrified and buttoned up and went out. I've regretted it ever since, may I say, because he seemed quite nice! Twenty years ago there'd have been no doubt. I'd have been delighted.

14 A remodelled life

John was born in 1917 on Tyneside into a working-class family. He 'fled' to London when he was fifteen and got a job as a dancer in a chorus. For some time he was 'kept' by richer, older men and offers a wealth of detail about various aspects of the gay scene during the inter-war years. He fought in the army during the Second World War and later became a civil servant, a model of respectability.

I was actually born in Tyneside and went to school there. I always wanted to dance, which of course was absolutely unheard of where I came from. So, to cut a long story short, I fled when I was fifteen, after my mother died, and came to London. I've always been gay, except that it wasn't called gay in those days. One used to say, are you 'so'? Or he's *comme ça*, if you were higher up, or TBH [to be had].

I got involved in hotel life first of all. I got a job as a pageboy. Then I became involved with the theatre and I went on a couple of tours as a member of the chorus.

I didn't actually go on the game but, when I first came to London, I was introduced to somebody called Tommy and he had a flat in central London. He used to have 'friends' who used to call on him for tea and he would invite his 'friends' and pair them off. Presents used to change hands, so I suppose really you'd say I was a call boy for a while. This was in 1936–7.

Tommy would invite you to tea and you were introduced to gentlemen and then he'd discreetly leave. His clients were MPs, doctors, lawyers and professional gentlemen. They paid Tommy and then he paid the boy. Very delicately done. If he knew that you didn't have any firm attachments he would sort of say, Would you like to come and have a glass of sherry next week? I've got somebody coming who you might like. Could I have a photograph of you? he used to say. And he had an album of photographs.

During the thirties the whole of the queer world was divided into castes, right. There were the boys on the game, there were the boys who weren't on the game but who were amenable (pick somebody up, and go and have dinner with them, go to bed with them), and there were the 'kept' boys. And then, of course, there were the 'steamers' or punters themselves. That's the old-fashioned term for them. I first heard it when I was about thirteen and somebody said, oh he's a steamer, he'll give you half a crown, you see. They tended to be older and better off and, of course, in high society.

You weren't just taken out because you were pretty, you were taken out because you were a pretty face in the first place, but you weren't taken out the second time because you were just a pretty face. What a lot of people do is they find a boy they like and then they try to remodel him. Which is stupid. Nobody's tried to remodel me. I've remodelled myself, but nobody's tried to remodel me.

I was a bit troubled by my homosexuality when I was very young. I had a schoolteacher who was quite young, and I thought he was the most lovely thing that had ever happened. And as I was very good at figures and I knew about taking scores at cricket, I went away one weekend with him. I had permission from the family to go with him, to do a weekend cricket match. And I went to bed with him. I went to bed with him. He had no chance. I mean the whole point is it's awful, because if anything had happened he would have got into trouble. And it wasn't him, it was me. I mean how can you resist a twelve-year-old groping you? What do you do? He was only a temporary teacher. I loved him, he was absolutely lovely.

I learned 'palari' when I was in the theatre, but it was a common language. It was originally the language of circus people. There are bits of pig Latin as well. For instance, face is

ecaf. Well that's just face backwards. Riah, that's hair backwards. But you have other things, hands are lappers, legs are
lallipegs, breasts are jubes, eyes are ocals or opals. It's died out
now. I think it was Bruce Forsyth who did a whole song in the
palari, and then of course Kenneth Williams and Hugh
Paddick in *Beyond Our Ken*. So it really became like everything
else, everybody does it. So there's no more mystery about it.
But then it used to be great fun. It was common only among a
certain class in the gay world. It was usually people like myself
who were in the chorus, the common end of the structure,
who used it.

I used to belong to all the clubs, it was half-a-crown a year to
be a member. They were mostly around Soho, there were a
couple in Mayfair, but it was mostly around Soho, Dean Street,
Romilly Street. Mostly only a room up a staircase. Usually run by
a woman for homosexual customers. That's how one used to
meet people. You had to show a card, and she got to know you
eventually. You got a membership through another member or
you were taken and made a member. The famous one, of
course, was a club in Panton Street, and also the Music Box.

These were open during the early part of the Second World
War. But there were lots of them, there was the Sphinx, the
Careless Stork, Sandy's, the Festival, and Sonia's in a basement
in Dean Street, and run by an enormous fat woman called Sonia.
They opened at three o'clock in the afternoon; three 'till eleven.
There were also gay pubs. There was the Cavour Bar, which was
elegant and had the most wonderful staircase, in Leicester
Square. It used to sweep down with a long bar, and there was
also the long bar at the Trocadero, which was more or less gay.
There was the French House, which has always been gay, York
Minster in Soho, the Golden Lion, the Fitzroy, and of course
the Running Horse in Shepherd Market.

There isn't a place now in London like the Coventry Street
Corner House. The first floor used to be known as the Lily
Pool. One used to go to tea, and you dressed up. It wasn't to
pick up anybody specifically, it was to do the tables and listen
to the gossip. It was a great garden party atmosphere. It was
completely queer, the whole thing. The waitresses knew you,

and, if you were a regular, they saved a table for you. There did use to be pick-ups, you know, that sort of thing, mostly by introduction.

There were gay marriages going on too. One would get into drag as a bride and somebody would marry them and have a party. There was much more socialising in those days than there is now. Mind you, I don't go out into the scene now, because the scene bores me. And if you go into a place that's got a disco you can't talk to anybody. There's no sitting around gossiping over your cup of tea or a glass of wine or a bottle of beer. I don't know, maybe there is talking among the youngsters, I don't know. But if you're over thirty you're bloody old. I think some of these kids don't know what they're missing.

I used to give parties like mad. When we were living in rooms we used to have pay parties. Or people would bring cut sand-wiches so thick nobody would eat them, and would bring a bottle. Have bottle parties. There was always a party somewhere. There was a saucer on the table for the odd shilling to pay for the gas or the electric, actually to pay for the rent! I had a very understanding landlady. If I had a friend back, she'd say, you had a friend on Wednesday, it's another two shillings on the rent. Everybody did cottaging. I always remember the advice I was given by an old friend who said, if you're going to do the cottages do one at a time. And always take a bus to the next one. Not like some of the silly queens I hear who go in and out just like the weather man. There were class cottages, of course. But most of them are closed, all these lovely places we had. All gone, and the tin chapels too.

The cottages were raided the whole time, with *agents provoca-teur* just the same as today. The boys on the Dilly got to know the plain-clothes people. There were some in Newcastle, where we used to congregate on Saturday nights, a whole crowd of us laughing and giggling, and somebody would suddenly scream, here's the carriage and pair. That was two policemen on a motorbike and sidecar, who used to chase us.

I once got the clap. And that was dreadful, but it was frontal clap. I was sixteen. You went in and they put you in a stall with a can and a tube and a thing you had to stick up your cock and let fluid go in, to wash yourself out. If you had anal clap I think you fled the country! I don't think you did anything, quite honestly. I used to go twice yearly for blood tests privately. Birthday and Christmas, my own present to myself. You found out about the clinic from the enamel notices in public lavatories. It advised to report immediately.

When I was very young we got to know of a queer doctor. If there was anything wrong like a rash or anything like that, which might have been crabs or scabies, we always used to go to him. He was very discreet and very good and very cheap. In London there was a gay doctor, who had his rooms in Harley Street, and we all used to go to him, and he was very expensive. I used to go to him twice a year for blood tests and a smear. An anal smear, just in case. But he was expensive. Discreet, comfortable, the fashionable gay doctor.

The bravest man in the world I know is Quentin Crisp. Even we used to cross the road and walk on the other side when he was coming towards us! It's a terrible thing to say, but he was persecuted by us as much as he was persecuted by everybody else. If we came upon him in a covered place, like a pub or a club, we would talk to him, but I can only talk about myself, I've seen him coming towards me down the street and I've crossed the road.

There was a Bloomsbury character, a woman, and she was a great friend of his, she was a great friend to all the gays, the original faggots' moll. She had absolutely no compunction about it at all, he was her friend. If anybody insulted him they insulted her and she used to lash out with her handbag.

Homosexuality in the East End of London had always been absolutely accepted. I mean going back to my early days, we used to go to the East End occasionally to one of the pubs where the mums and dads used to go. And they used to refer to the boys by their camp name, Hello Lola, love. How are you dear? You going to give us a song? The East End of London, which had very tightly knit families living in their streets of terraced houses, in and out of one another's, they knew about their sons and it was accepted.

After I met my lover, he took me everywhere with him. I was

never kept in the background. He wore me like a badge. He was one who had a penchant for the working class. I used to do the housework, until eventually I had someone come in, but he was a slob. I mean I used to do his clothes and things like that because he used to leave everything lying about the place. He was the untidiest man I've ever met! Ash down himself and everything. I used to get him dressed to go off to work and he'd look an unmade bed in five minutes!

We never had an exclusive relationship. He never stopped. He was the most promiscuous man I ever met. I didn't mind because I knew that the relationship was firm, and so it really didn't matter.

He thought that with the background I came from, I should be a rabid socialist. In fact I'm a bloody blue conservative! Only the rich can afford to be socialist. If you've got plenty of money and you're living in comfort you can afford to be a socialist. If you've got no money and are looking at squalor you can't afford to be anything else but a conservative. Truly, I mean it must be.

It wasn't until recently really that I ever took the law against homosexuality as being a stumbling block. I don't think it's made much difference to anything, quite honestly. It's only made people more wary about going to bed with younger people. At one time it didn't matter how old you were if you went to bed with somebody, you were still in trouble. But now you're told that you mustn't have anybody unless they're twenty-one.

You'd have somebody who was say an eighteen- or nineteen-year-old living with an older person who knew the boyfriend of another one who were living together and these two would sometimes have a ding-dong together. The two mistresses would have a ding-dong together. But it was all kept in the family. My knowledge might have been constricted, but there were very few same-age couples.

Even the ongoing relationships were based on money. The boys who went to live with these older people became dependent. A husband-wife relationship. Quite a lot of them went on for ever you know. There were a lot of same-age friends, but they were non-sexual friends, you would just have them round to tea or something.

The attitude was, oh no, I couldn't sleep with her dear, you know, she's a queen! A queen was supposed to be passive and effeminate and young. An old queen was rather frowned upon. But there were old queens, of course. I mean people don't change their sexual habits just because they were older.

No, there was a great thing about putting people into compartments. Active. Passive. People used to say to me, what do you do? And I say, well I can change my mind. What do you like? I mean it's a bloody stupid question to ask.

I think the introduction of the American queens over here during the Second World War changed a lot of homosexual people's attitudes towards sex. The Americans were much more inventive. They also had an effect on the rates in the rent boy market. I think the rates were £1, in those early days. But the Americans ruined that market, it went up to $10. Generally I think there were changes because people were away from home, and I think it was because of the blackout - there was a great deal more fumbling going on in cottages than ever.

I was six years and a hundred and twelve days in the army and ravishing it was too! And I stayed. I could have got out, but I didn't want to. Didn't have time for sex in the army. Though there used to be a lot to be had. I used to play hard to get, which is nicer! The attitude to homosexuality in the army was protective. They used to send me up like mad. But if any stranger did it he used to be kicked to death, you know. I was regarded as rather strange. I have never been particularly 'femme', but my turn of phrase and attitude was regarded as rather strange. I was a sort of Evelyn Home to the boys you know, comfort for the troops! They didn't confess their homosexuality to me, but they 'used' me sexually occasionally. They always swore their undying love, you know! Mm.

After the war, when my lover and I split up, I went into the civil service. I did quite well, actually. I became respectable!

I still get going with people occasionally. I had this boyfriend for about three years, but he was so bloody possessive he had to go. I tried to explain to him that friends take a hell of a time to make and you've got to work at keeping them. And he resented the fact that I had some. I haven't got a lot of friends, I've got a lot of acquaintances, but the few friends I have I've had all my life.

Only when complete and total acceptance is given and when the law is changed completely and utterly, so that, for instance, people who have settled down together are treated as man and wife as far as the law is concerned, in terms of inheritance, will we have equality. That is what should be fought for, not the right to hold hands in the street. We've always held hands in the street if we wanted to. I mean, we linked arms in the thirties.

Mind you, I am glad something like Gay Switchboard now exists. In my day there wasn't anything like that. You just found out about things, and if you were vulnerable you found out the wrong way. And now you don't have to, you can be put on the right lines by lots of places and people. You had your mentor, you had your elder friend in my day, but that was all.

I don't like the word gay. It puts a sort of carnival atmosphere about the whole thing, which it isn't. And which it shouldn't be. There should be a better word for it. Why should there be even 'queer' for it? I mean, why should there? We're no different to anyone else. All this business about being far more intelligent, far more artistic, far more this, and far more that, is a load of old rubbish. We might be far more 'conscious', but only because we have to be.

I'm not saying this in any sense of bravado or anything like that, but there's not one day I've ever regretted being queer or gay. No, no regrets whatever. I have nothing but gratitude for the people I've met. And nothing but admiration for most of them. And those I dislike I've told so. I mean it's as simple as that.

15 A professional's life

Tony, born in 1921, was brought up in Hampshire during the inter-war years. After his parents split up and his mother died, he lived with relatives and he attended a boarding school. He moved to London at the age of sixteen, partly to escape the bank career his relatives planned for him, and partly because he wanted to become a dancer. In fact he never took up dancing but became a 'professional', or male prostitute. This remained his career up to this interview, conducted when he was in his late fifties.

I was born in Hampshire. And I lived a quite ordinary life except that what really brought me to London was my father left my mother. My mother then died and I went to live with relatives. We didn't speak the same language at all, and I was somebody that liked music and dancing and that sort of thing. My uncle was in a bank, and wanted me to go into that. It ended in a long argument and I picked up my savings and just took off for London at sixteen. That was two years before the war.

I'd had plenty of homosexual feelings. Not so much actually at school. I did know boys that I was aware that I liked better than others, and certainly boys better than girls. The basic thing you have is a sort of feeling, you could kiss that man but you couldn't kiss that woman, you know, that sort of thing.

I remember shocking my relatives when I was young, being innocent. They were talking about various things, they were what I call country people, they wouldn't know what a homosexual person was, in fact as far as I could make out even their own sex relations were all done in the dark! I remember saying once, well actually I could kiss a man or fall in love with a man much more than a woman. And there was a deadly silence you see, and I didn't realise why there should be this silence, I mean I was just speaking naturally. I think probably they suddenly thought, hello, there's something wrong with him. Perhaps he should go and see a doctor. Anyway it never came to anything and, although the offspring of my relations are still alive, we've never kept in touch.

I just came to London with the idea of going into the theatre as a dancer really. I knew that the only break was as a chorus person. What I didn't realise was that the two years before the war were going to be harder than when the war came, because when the war came all your main trained people went into the services, and providing you knew your right foot from your left you could get a job. But for the first two years I had to find the cheapest digs.

I remember finding a place in Bloomsbury and it wasn't till later I suddenly realised that the landlord was awfully kind to me! He never made any physical move, but I realise now that really he was hoping, perhaps, I would respond. Well, frankly it didn't really worry me at that particular moment, although I was aware of the usual things. I used to like to handle myself and that sort of thing, and sometimes when one used to go to the gents you'd see people doing exactly the same and I suppose you automatically joined in. I wasn't conscious ever of it being something wrong or illegal or anything like that. That side of it didn't come up at all.

I just felt I needed to do it, and going about, having coffees and things, I used to see people that I found attractive to me but I took it quite normally. I wasn't aware that there was such a thing. You see they didn't teach sex at school in those days, and I suppose in a sort of way, if I'd had a normal mother/father relation, dad would have taken me aside and told me about what they call the birds and the bees or whatever it is, I don't quite know what birds and bees do! But one had to find it out for oneself.

I was aware when I was at school, I was at boarding school, that there was one prefect that I liked very much and he obviously liked me, because he used to give me special privileges.

You had to do ordinary jobs like delivering the papers to their studies and I found myself rushing through the others to get to his, so that by the time the bell went there was plenty of time with him. It was the first time I suppose that somebody reached out and kissed me and, well I was delighted, but he never went any further than that. I did the usual, masturbated, two doing it together, doing it to each other, but there was no talk about being gay or doing it with women. I don't think quite honestly they were any more different than I was. This prefect I'm talking about, although we got to the kissing stage, nothing actually physically happened that way. And yet I saw him in the holidays, and we used to go to the theatre together. I know he must have liked women and I suppose now he's got about fifteen children.

I became aware of homosexuality fairly soon after coming to London when I was sixteen. I suppose really through having to eke out one's savings as it were, and that I hadn't got enough money to go and be trained as a dancer. Most of the shows at that time wanted fully trained people. I used to go to auditions and didn't get parts. So it was a question of knowing what to do.

I was made aware of the sex side, as far as I remember, when I met other people. I wasn't conscious that they were even gay, let alone, what do you call it, male prostitutes.

I used to meet them in Soho cafés. We'd talk. One friend was called Roger, I think it was. I used to meet him in there, hello and that, and we'd sit down. He used to say to me, any luck?, and I said no, I really don't know what I'm going to do. That's when he more or less told me there are other ways of what are called making a bit of money. I don't know whether he thought I was too innocent. I was conscious of camp and I liked him, but nothing in that way, and he used to sit in this café with me. Sometimes these very nice gentlemen would come in and say, hello Roger, are you ready? He would get up and say, I must go now, my friend's called.

One night, this friend called for him, and he had a friend with him, and they said they were going out for some drinks and dinner. He said, well perhaps your friend would like to come along, that's me, you see. Anyway this Roger did say to me, well we must just go to the gents first. Anyway, he took me down and he said, you do know what it means, don't you? And I said, well I take it it means that he'll want to sort of kiss me or something after. He says, well he may want to do more than that! But he's very nice and he'd already told me he got little presents and that sort of thing. And that's more or less how one sort of slipped into it.

I did say to him right away, well look I'd heard about being buggered and I knew I wanted to be more active than passive.

So I went out with the two that evening. Actually nothing much happened that evening. We went out to somewhere else in London, and then Roger said something about, I must go back home, and said goodnight. I said, well I must go too. And so the gentleman and I left together and then he said, well perhaps you'd like to come back to my place and have a drink. When we got back he talked about it and he asked me right out, he said, tell me, are you... ? Well, I think the word was 'rent' in those days. I remember saying, well I haven't been but I'm ready to be. Anyway I spent the night there. He then asked me if I'd like to stay there and sort of look after the flat while he was out, and I remember saying, well you've only just met me. It didn't occur to me.... Mind you things weren't quite as dangerous as they are today.

I spent three months with him. It was very pleasant, and I was 'kept', if you know, and then he was called up. By that time I knew much more about it, I knew the places to go. I'd been taken to clubs with him. There was one at the back of the Leicester Square cinema, I can't remember the name of the street. It was rather elegant, a nice big room and a grand piano, and very, very nice people.

You had to be a member and I used to go there with him. Mind you, don't forget, I was sixteen-and-a-half and that sort of thing, and I couldn't be made a member because he didn't want to give away that I was only sixteen-and-a-half. I used to try and make myself look a bit older. I think a lot of them knew, you went in, you signed them in, and I think their attitude was, oh they weren't going to turn him down for drinks and I think they shut their eyes to it. If they were raided they'd say, well, we didn't know he was sixteen-and-a-half, but nothing like that ever came up, I never had that sort of trouble.

Only once have I ever been in a club when the police raided, but they only took names. Some people panic, and think you're going to be carted off in a black maria. It is more intimidation.

I'd met a lot of other people, friends of his, who automatically, being seventeen, fancied one. I didn't do anything about it. I had that thing that we all have of wanting to belong to somebody. But when he was called up, and subsequently killed in the war, well an awful lot of those people immediately pounced on one, you're free now. I was not bandied around, but I went with quite a lot of people. I knew I was eventually going to be called up and I didn't see any point not enjoying myself as much as possible till then, to save some money for when I was called up. Then I could come out with enough to train to be a dancer properly. So for the two years I really let myself be prostituted around, and enjoyed it I must say.

I never saw myself as anything like the street boys. The first man I was with taught me everything. We used to go along Piccadilly and he'd say, now don't you ever do that. You'd see them being picked up. He said, you're better class than that, you're educated. That's for the silly little queens. I'd learnt by then there were two bars, one in Piccadilly you went straight into, and one in Leicester Square called the Cavour. It went in for an awful lot of chorus boys and that's really why I went, because I thought I might land a job. And of course the Ritz Bar.

I remember thinking at the time that whereas a prostitute, even a female prostitute, has a bad reputation for wanting to get it over quickly, get as much money as possible, I thought no, if I'm going to do it, I'm going to enjoy it. Because I do like the body and I mean there's hardly anybody I can't touch happily. I will always say well, if they were going to give me so much money, it's not going to be in and out as quickly as possible. The first man said, you will find that some of my friends will want to take over from me. He taught me an awful lot about how to do it. If they want it all over in five minutes, that's not your problem and some people won't want everything, so have various rates for it. Have a basic one just for the basic, and anything else extra. Add extra for staying the night.

In the old days I used to ask, are you active? Are you passive? It was very much more slotted. Now it's not nearly as slotted.

The only time I came across somebody straight was perhaps if they were a bit drunk or something. And I'm not very fond of drunks at the best of times. At parties you might perhaps find yourself on the settee with a drink and somebody would say, come on, be nice to me, and put his hand on you, and I used to let them get on with it. But I never liked spending a night with anybody who I knew was a bit drunk. I used to always get up and go early in the morning. Before they came to and found out what they'd done and been sorry for themselves, although I never had any problem with them.

I never had any brushes with the law either. I think mainly because, being educated, I was sensible enough not to do things in parks and things like that. I really wasn't mad about the other rent boys, they were the ones that used to call themselves by girls' names like Lucy and Annette. They were what I call the really camp queens. I don't like saying that, but that's what they behaved like. Those were the ones that used to stroll up and down Piccadilly.

I never quite understood that, and I still don't quite understand it. They weren't dressed as women, but they walked in a womanly way and they dyed their hair. I often used to wonder who really wants to go with them because if you pick up a male who thinks he's got a woman, well when you get back he's going to find he hasn't. I mean to say, it is not going to be very satisfactory all round is it? But then I would never act like a woman. I enjoyed doing it and I made it quite clear what I would do and what I wouldn't do, and what I said I would do I would do.

I didn't get up in the morning with the idea of going out and seeing how many men I could have in a day. Half of them were very bored with just going to a club and sitting there waiting to pick up somebody for a one-night stand. If they found somebody who was interesting and they could go to the theatre with them and go out to dinner, like me, then we both benefited by it. I used to see a lot of them socially even if sometimes I never went back with them.

I didn't have regulars, although there were one or two. There was one married man, for instance, who lived in the country and was only up once every fortnight, I think it was on a Wednesday or something, and he liked me to try and be free on that Wednesday. I've been known to have one in the afternoon and one in the evening, or perhaps even one in the early evening and one in the late evening.

If I knew them they paid at the end. I never really picked up anybody in the streets. I never stood on street corners, I'd always go to a bar that I knew of, and sometimes not intending to it would happen, another time you want it to happen and it doesn't.

Whereas the general impression is that professionals like to do as little for as much as possible, I find so often that it's the other way round, that it's sometimes the client that wants as much as he can get for as little. I've got a working-class man at the moment, he's a welder and gets £150 a week or something like that, and he would do everything to try and get me, and just because he can only fit it in his lunch hour he doesn't see why he should pay the same as somebody else! It is extraordinary. The period I am talking about though is mainly the thirties and during the Second World War.

During the war I wouldn't say there were blackouts, because you had blue lights everywhere and everybody carried a torch with a bit of tissue paper on it. I don't know how much went on in doorways. Only once, in my whole life, have I ever done anything like that out-of-doors. I met somebody in a bar and I think he said, can I come back with you? And I said, well I can't, because I only had this very small room. We hadn't got anywhere because he was staying with friends. So anyway, I said, well I'll walk home with you. He madly wanted to suck me off and suddenly he got me into a doorway and did it. Well, it wasn't until it was over that I suddenly thought it would only have taken a policeman to come along. In a sort of way, when I look back upon it, I didn't think of it as anything criminal. It happened quick and there was a certain excitement about it, but it wasn't something I would make a habit of.

One was aware of the law. I used to see those 'Piccadilly boys', as we used to call them, sometimes getting arrested and being taken away in black marias. I used to think in terms, well, that will never happen to me, because I don't do that sort of thing. It never occurred to me that there might be detectives undercover in a club. I used to think of it as it is now, perfectly legal providing you mind your own business. I don't think I was really made aware of the law until years later when the Montagu case came up. Then you realised that you could be had up for something that had happened three years before.

I knew it I suppose. I suppose I must have done, but it's like a lot of things that are illegal. I mean we all stole sugar off tables and things like that during the war. But one called it pilfering, not stealing.

I've never felt guilty about being homosexual. I'm not going to say I feel proud of being a homosexual. No, I don't feel proud, but I'm not ashamed. It's not like taking up golf, you'll go with men instead of women. I suggest that a heterosexual will say, oh so and so's queer, but a homosexual has a perfect right to say a heterosexual is queer, to him. I said this once to a het, I said, you're queer to me as far as I'm concerned because I'm doing what's natural. I haven't flaunted it, I just accepted it.

I still have customers now. I've got an American coming over here this June, and I haven't met him yet, but it's word of mouth from an American who was over here last year. That's the best way to do it because they say what you're like, they say what you'll do and whether you're interesting. I do go very much on word of mouth. But if it was somebody I just met, for example, if I was sitting having a drink and they got talking and say what do you do, I would just say, well I'm a professional, and we would take it from there.

Index

Other Rivers Oram titles by Jeffrey Weeks

Against Nature
Essays on history, sexuality and identity
Jeffrey Weeks

These influential essays record a particular personal, intellectual and political journey which will find echoes in a range of contexts and disciplines.

Sexual identities, Jeffrey Weeks argues, are both historically invented and essential in day-to-day life. They are constructed in a traceable history but are the crucial means through which we negotiate the hazards of contemporary lives. They are necessary fictions.

The essays explore a number of interrelated themes from the making of homosexual identities to the politics and values of the period we think of as 'post-modern'.

'There are few people better qualified to promote sanity...Weeks writes with clarity and passionate conviction...it would be difficult not to profit from this elegant and controlled discussion.'
Diarmid MacCulloch, *Times Higher Education Supplement*

'...as befits Weeks's venerable status, he's come out with a collection [which] illustrates both the breakthroughs and the impasses he has encountered in striving to write a new kind of history.'
William Kendrick, *Village Voice*

ISBN 1 85489 028 X (hardback) £30.00
ISBN 1 85489 004 2 (paperback) £9.95

The Lesser Evil and the Greater Good

The theory and politics of social diversity
Jeffrey Weeks (editor)

As we come to terms with ideas of fragmentation, difference, plurality and contingency, is it still possible to find common human standards? This book draws on a range of writings from Kant and Weber to Rorty and Foucault to address this question, embracing discussions of post-Marxism, feminist theory, the new 'queer' politics, ecology and race.

In examining the conflict between the relative and the universal, the authors explore the possibility of establishing political values that can validate both diversity and wider solidarities.

The Lesser Evil and the Greater Good takes the reader on an illuminating journey through the maze of contemporary post-modern debates. It clarifies the main issues at stake and demonstrates that an active rethinking of politics and ethics is not only desirable but possible.

Illustrating the complexities of the challenges facing a theory and politics of social diversity, the authors suggest opportunities for a new political imaginary, which can hold in balance both a respect for difference and recognition of common concerns: the lesser evil *and* the greater good.

Contributors include, Chetan Bhatt, John Bird, Peter Jowers, Ernesto Laclau, Rosemary McKechnie, Frank Mort, Anne Phillips, Anna Marie Smith, Judith Squires, Jem Thomas, Simon Thompson, Sean Watson and Ian Welsh.

'Will take you to the outermost frontiers of current debates in post-modernism and post-Marxism'
Chartist

'Provocative....It is very rare to come across a collection which has no dud pieces, yet the consistent quality of thought and ethos of engagement exhibited in this volume make this such an occasion....This deserves widespread scrutiny and discussion.'
Sociology

ISBN 1 85489 054 9 (hardback) £30.00
ISBN 1 85489 055 7 (paperback) £11.95